# CONTENTS    VALOUR IN THE AIR

9

52

68

110

*Andy Hay/www.flyingart.co.uk*

34

**SECOND EDITION** - This special publication was originally released in 2017 as Valour in the Air

**Valour in the Air**

**Editor** Stephen Bridgewater.  **Sub Editor** Rebecca Gibbs.  **Proof Reading** Jamie Ewan & Richard Freail.  **Design and Layout** Paul Silk  **Cover Design** Steve Donovan
**Group CEO** Adrian Cox  **Publisher** Mark Elliott  **Chief Publishing Officer** Jonathan Jackson  **Head of Production** Janet Watkins
**Distribution** Seymour Distribution Ltd +44 (0)20 7429 4000. **Printing** Precision Colour Printing Ltd, Telford, Shropshire. TF7 4QQ.

*All images via the Key Publishing Archive unless stated*

**ISBN is 978 1 913295 78 3**

**Published by Key Publishing Ltd, PO Box 100, Stamford, Lincs PE19 1XQ.**
**Tel: +44 (0) 1780 755131. Website: www.keypublishing.com**

 © Key Publishing Ltd 2020

# The Victoria Cross

## The Victoria Cross traces its history back to the Crimean War and has become one of the most admired and prized medals in military history.

The Victoria Cross (VC) is the highest award within the United Kingdom honours system. Since it was introduced in 1856 the VC has been awarded 1,358 times to 1,355 individual recipients.

The VC is awarded for gallantry 'in the face of the enemy' and can be presented to a person of any military rank in any service and to civilians under military command-although no civilian has received the award since 1879.

The Crimean War (1853-1856) was one of the first conflicts fought amidst modern reporting and the dispatches sent back by *The Times*' war correspondent, William Howard Russell, described many acts of unrewarded bravery.

At this point there was no official standardised system for the recognition of gallantry within the British armed forces. Sometimes senior officers would be awarded medals; occasionally junior grades were presented with the Order of the Bath or promotions while a Mention in Despatches existed for acts of lesser gallantry.

Meanwhile, other European countries had awards that did not discriminate against class or rank; France awarded the Légion d'honneur (Legion of Honour) and the Netherlands gave the Military Order of William. As a result, and partly in response to pressure from the general public, Queen Victoria issued a Warrant to constitute a new medal on January 29, 1856. Eligibility was backdated to 1854 to recognise all acts of valour during the Crimean War and the new medal would be awarded irrespective of birth or class.

A single company of jewellers, Hancocks of London, has been responsible for the production of every VC awarded since its inception. The medal consists of a bronze cross pattée bearing the crown of Saint Edward surmounted by a lion with the inscription 'FOR VALOUR'. The medal is usually worn with a crimson ribbon but those issued to naval personnel before 1918 came with a dark blue ribbon

## Crimean Cannons

A single company of jewellers, Hancocks of London, has been responsible for the production of every VC awarded since its inception.

When the medals were announced it was widely reported that they would be struck from the metal of melted down cascabels from Russian cannons captured during the Siege of Sevastopol. However, metallurgy tests and x-rays of medals during the last 20 years have determined that the metal is actually much older and likely of Chinese descent.

There are a number of theories about their ancestry and some have suggested that they may have been Chinese guns that had been captured by the Russians – but there had been no hostilities between the two nations for almost 200 years prior to the cannons' capture at Sevastopol. A more likely theory is that when the original smelters were sent to the repository to collect the metal, they returned with cannons captured during the First Opium War (1839-1842).

Today, the barrels of the cannons are on display at the Royal Artillery Museum at Woolwich, London and the remaining portion of the only remaining cascabel (the subassembly of a muzzle-loading cannon) is stored in a vault at MoD Donnington near

**Bomber Command aircrew won the lion's share of the VCs awarded to aircrew during World War Two. Although the famous Lancaster topped the tables the Blenheim, Wellington, Manchester and Hampden fleets also produced pilots and crew with the incredible bravery necessary to receive a Victoria Cross**

◄ Many of the aircrew who were awarded the VC had already earned an impressive haul of other medals. This group belonged to Group Captain Leonard Cheshire and includes (left to right) the Victoria Cross, Distinguished Service Order and two bars, Distinguished Flying Cross, 1939-45 Star, Air Crew Europe Star with Atlantic clasp, Burma Star, Defence Medal, War Medal 1939-45 with Mentioned in Dispatches insignia, Queen Elizabeth II Coronation Medal and the Queen Elizabeth II Silver Jubilee Medal

Just over 30 years separated the first and the last aviators to receive the VC. On May 22, 1915 William Rhodes-Moorhouse (left) was the first aviator to be awarded the medal and on Robert Hampton Gray (right) was the last pilot of World War Two to be credited with a VC; this relating to his actions on August 9, 1945. Other pilots were subsequently awarded the medal for action earlier in the war; their stories often coming to light once prisoners of war had been repatriated and enemy logs studied

Telford, Shropshire. It is thought that the remaining 22lb (10kg) of metal is sufficient to produce 80 to 85 more VCs.

The medal itself is a bronze cross pattée, 1.6in (41mm) high and 1.4in (36mm) wide, carrying both the crown of Saint Edward surmounted by a lion and the inscription 'FOR VALOUR'.

Interestingly, the inscription was originally to have been 'FOR THE BRAVE', until it was changed on the recommendation of Queen Victoria, who pointed out that it implied that not all men in battle were brave.

Each VC hangs from a suspension bar decorated with laurel leaves on the front and the recipient's name, rank, number and unit on the reverse. The back of the medal features a circular panel on which the date of the act for which it was awarded is engraved.

The original specification for the award stated that the ribbon should be crimson red for army recipients and

dark blue for naval recipients, however the dark blue ribbon was abolished soon after the formation of the Royal Air Force on April 1, 1918.

## Recipients

The Victoria Cross is presented for '... most conspicuous bravery, or some daring or pre-eminent act of valour or self-sacrifice, or extreme devotion to duty in the presence of the enemy' and the first awards ceremony was held on June 26, 1857, when Queen Victoria invested 62 of the 111 Crimean recipients in Hyde Park, London.

A recommendation for the VC is normally issued by an officer and has to be supported by three witnesses. After vetting, the recommendation is then laid

► Many of the men that received a VC are now recognised with 'Blue Plaques' on their childhood homes or schools – this is Albert Ball's plaque at Grantham School▼ *Steve Bridgewater*

before the monarch who approves the award with his or her signature before the award is promulgated in the London Gazette.

The VC was extended to colonial troops in 1867 and the first posthumous awards were granted on August 8, 1902.

In the 160 years since the first VC was presented, the medal has been awarded 1,358 times to 1,355 individual recipients but only 15 have been given out since the end of World War Two.

## Aeronautical Heroes

The advent of aerial warfare during the Great War meant that pilots of the Royal Flying Corps (RFC) and, later, the RAF were putting themselves in grave danger on an almost daily basis. It was therefore inevitable that the new breed of aerial knights would soon feature within the ranks of VC holders.

On April 26, 1915 William Barnard Rhodes-Moorhouse became the first aviator to be awarded the VC, albeit posthumously, after his Royal Aircraft Factory BE.2 was downed in Belgium whilst bombing a railway junction.

By the end of the Great War, some 19 members of aircrew had been awarded the VC for their gallantry and by the end of World War Two the total number of aviators who received the award stood at 51. This is their story.

❖

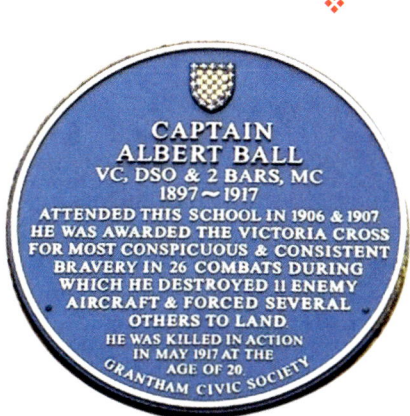

# The First of the Few

## Aviation pioneer William Rhodes-Moorhouse was the first airman to be awarded the Victoria Cross. His story is one of victory and tragedy

William Barnard Rhodes-Moorhouse (September 26, 1887 – April 27, 1915) was born in Rokeby, North Yorkshire to parents of New Zealand descent.

William's mother, Mary Ann Rhodes, had been bequeathed a legacy from her father that meant she was the richest woman in New Zealand prior to relocating to Great Britain in 1883. As a result, William was sent to Harrow School as well as Trinity Hall, Cambridge. However, he neglected his studies in favour of his love of engineering as well as racing cars and motorcycles.

In 1909, at the age of 22, Rhodes-Moorhouse decided to take private flying lessons and soon gained his pilot's certificate (No 147).

He went on to design several flying machines for air races and some of the earliest aerial meetings, where he flew alongside the likes of T.O.M. Sopwith and Claude Graham-White.

Rhodes-Moorhouse's early attempts at creating a flying machine met with mixed results but in 1910 he teamed up with fellow aviation enthusiast James Radley to develop the successful 50hp Radley-Moorhouse monoplane. Later that year the pair sailed to the USA where they purchased a 50hp Gnome-

**William Barnard Rhodes-Moorhouse
(September 26, 1887 – April 27, 1915)**

powered Blériot XI aeroplane and entered a number of air races, winning several prizes before returning to Britain in February 1911.

Rhodes-Moorhouse was involved in an accident on April 7, 1912 when the aircraft he was flying crashed at Portholme Airfield in Huntingdonshire. His jaw was damaged and he was fitted with a full set of dentures to replace his broken and missing teeth, but he was clearly undeterred from flying as just two months later he came second in the inaugural Aerial Derby, which was held at Brooklands, Surrey on June 8.

Later the same month he also married Linda Morritt, a school friend of his sister, who proved to be equally fearless and quickly grew to love flying .

## Record Breaker

In fact, just two months after their marriage the pair crossed the English Channel in a Breguet biplane on August 4. The fragile aircraft also carried the Royal Aero Club's John Ledeboer and Rhodes-Moorhouse therefore became the first person to successfully fly two passengers across the Channel.

The flight ended in a crash landing in bad weather near Ashford, Kent, which destroyed the aircraft but did not appear to harm those on board. Reports suggest Rhode-Moorhouse had been ferrying the Breguet from Belgium to Great Britain in order to take part in the Military Aircraft Trials at Larkhill on Salisbury Plain. He was certainly listed as one of the pilots taking part in the trials on August 6 but it is unclear which aircraft he flew, or if he flew at all.

In fact it appears that Rhodes-Moorhouse flew very little after his post-Channel crossing crash landing and

**Rhodes-Moorhouse was an aviation pioneer and learned to fly at the age of 22. He went on to design several flying machines for air races and then teamed up with fellow aviation enthusiast James Radley to develop the successful 50hp Radley-Moorhouse monoplane**

**By March 1915 there was such a need for war pilots that Rhodes-Moorhouse's requests to be moved to the frontline could be ignored no longer and he was assigned to 2 Sqn at Merville flying the unarmed Royal Aircraft Factory BE.2**

The 'Biggles Biplane' is a replica BE.2c operated by Matthew Boddington and flown as part of the Great War Display Team. The aircraft, which is registered G-AWYI and is based on a Tiger Moth, is currently painted in a scheme representing Rhodes-Moorhouse's '687' *Steve Bridgewater*

he appears to have decided that motor racing was infinitely safer!

## 'Doing his Bit'

When war broke out with Germany in August 1914, Rhodes-Moorhouse was keen to 'do his bit' and enlisted as a 2nd Lieutenant in the Royal Flying Corps (RFC).

He was initially based at Farnborough, Hampshire where he worked as an engineer servicing aero engines. Although he was keen to fly, and clearly had far more experience than many of his comrades, RFC rules forbade him due to his dentures.

Nonetheless, Rhodes-Moorhouse was determined not to remain ground-bound and soon he was flying on the quiet, ostensibly to conduct 'air tests' but also to build up his own experience on the most modern flying machines.

By March 1915 there was such a need for war pilots that his requests to be moved to the frontline could be ignored no longer and he was assigned to 2 Sqn at Merville near Calais, France flying the unarmed Royal Aircraft Factory BE.2.

During March and April he performed countless reconnaissance flights over the Western Front and was frequently fired at by anti-aircraft guns. On March 29, the centre section of his aircraft was hit by a shell but he landed safely and was clearly undeterred. Although the BE.2 was not equipped with guns, Rhodes-Moorhouse carried his service revolver and would try to manoeuvre himself and his observer close enough to fire upon any German aeroplanes encountered.

## Gallantry over Ypres

When the Second Battle of Ypres broke out in Belgium in April 1915, the combined French and British forces struggled to stem the German advances. On April 26 the RFC was ordered to bomb the German railway network at Kortrijk, Belgium to cut off the supply of armament and reinforcements between the Staden-Cortemarck-Roulers line and the railway stations at Thielt, Staden, Deynze and Inglemunster. This would be a perilous mission and although Rhodes-Moorhouse was due to go

The 'Biggles Biplane' BE.2c replica was commissioned in 1969 by the makers of the film 'Biggles Sweeps the Skies.' Designed by film model specialist David Boddington, it was built and flown in just 16 weeks by vintage aircraft specialist Charles Boddington at Sywell, Northamptonshire. Based on de Havilland Tiger Moth components the two brothers created an aeroplane that looked and flew just like the original. It was flown, crashed and then stored for 25 years in the USA before being returned to Sywell by Charles' son Matthew and rebuilt to fly *Steve Bridgewater*

Rhode-Moorhouse's usual aeroplane (No 492) had been damaged by enemy fire on a photoreconnaissance mission a few days before so he flew BE.2b 687 for the mission; the aircraft having been modified to carry a single 100lb high-explosive bomb mounted beneath the fuselage *Andy Hay/www.flyingart.co.uk*

## " Rhodes-Moorhouse refused medical attention until he'd reported the details of his sortie "

home on leave, he was requested to fly one final sortie.

He was under no illusion about the hazards or the importance of the mission and after writing letters to his mother, wife and four-month-old son, he took off solo at 3.05pm after 'quite an argument' with his observer, who wanted to go with him.

Rhode-Moorhouse's usual aeroplane (No 492) had been damaged by enemy fire on a photoreconnaissance mission a few days before so he flew BE.2 687 for the mission; the aircraft having been modified to carry a single 100lb (45kg) high-explosive bomb mounted beneath the fuselage.

Battling a strong headwind as well as intense anti-aircraft fire, Rhodes-Moorhouse pressed on towards the railway junction, where he had been instructed to drop his bomb from just below cloud level.

However, to guarantee hitting the tracks he descended to just 300ft (91m) amidst a torrent of ground fire that hit him in the thigh, abdomen and hand. Undeterred, he released his bomb right on target but his low altitude meant that the BE.2 was caught in the explosion and fragments ripped into the wood and canvas biplane, badly wounding the pilot.

Despite his injuries, Rhodes-Moorhouse nursed his battered aeroplane 35 miles (56km) back to base, where eyewitnesses saw him make a perfect landing at 4.12pm after just clearing the hedge. The injured and weak pilot had to be lifted from the cockpit by his observer and ground crew. His observer was amazed to see a line of bullet holes across the cockpit in which he would have sat. In total, the

aircraft had 95 holes from bullets and shrapnel and although he was faint and gravely injured, Rhodes-Moorhouse refused medical attention until he'd reported the details of his sortie.

Later that evening it became clear that a bullet had ripped his stomach to pieces and his injuries were so severe that he was unlikely to survive the night. He asked to see his flight commander, Maurice Blake, and showed him a photograph of Linda and their baby Willie, asking him to write to them and to his mother. If he was awarded a Military Cross (MC), he asked that it should go to his wife.

After a short sleep, he reportedly woke and said: "It's strange dying, Blake, old boy – unlike anything one has ever done before, like one's first solo flight."

Just after 1.00pm on April 27, he received Holy Communion from the chaplain and then a note arrived informing Rhodes-Moorhouse that he had been recommended for the Distinguished Service Order (DSO).

At 2.25pm, with a recently delivered letter from his wife on his pillow and his friend Blake at his side, Rhodes-Moorhouse died. He was 27.

The brave aviator was posthumously promoted to Lieutenant (backdated to the April 24) but it was largely Blake's lobbying that secured the VC for Rhodes-Moorhouse and, less than a month after he died, his award was announced in the *London Gazette* for 'most conspicuous bravery.' At the time, Field Marshal Sir John French, the British commander, said the pilot had been responsible for "the most important bomb dropped during the war so far". The award was the first VC

awarded to an airman.

William Rhodes-Moorhouse had asked to be buried at home and although it was not government policy for the dead to be repatriated, his body was returned to Britain on the orders of Lieutenant Colonel Hugh Trenchard, commander of the RFC's First Wing. As the Last Post sounded on May 5, William Rhodes-Moorhouse was laid to rest on the hillside overlooking his home at Parnham Park, near Beaminster, Dorset.

Just over 25 years later Rhodes-Moorhouse's son was laid to rest next to his father after being shot down and killed while flying a Hawker Hurricane with 601 Sqn RAF during the Battle of Britain. He had just claimed his 12th combat victory and been awarded the Distinguished Flying Cross (DFC). His father would have been proud. ❖

# The Great War VCs

## Just shy of 20 talented, brave and – on occasion – lucky pilots received Britain's most prestigious award for valour in the face of the enemy during World War One. This is the story of those gallant airmen.

Following on from Lieutenant William Rhodes-Moorhouse (see page 6), a further 18 airmen would be awarded the Victoria Cross before the Great War ended on November 11, 1918.

The first of these was Reginald Alexander John Warneford, who was born in Bengal, India on October 15, 1891 as the son of a British civil engineer. He was trained, variously, in England and India but at the age of 13 began an apprenticeship with the Merchant Marines before joining the British-India Steam Navigation Company.

Warneford was in Canada when war broke out in Europe and he immediately sailed for England and volunteered for the Army's '2nd Sportsman's Battalion.' However, within a month he applied to transfer to the Navy with a view to training to be a pilot in the Royal Naval Air Service (RNAS). He started flying at Hendon aerodrome near London before moving to Upavon, Wiltshire where he qualified on February 25, 1915 and was promoted to Flight Sub-lieutenant.

Warneford's first posting was to 2 Wing on the Isle of Sheppey in Kent where his 'over confidence' was of concern but on May 7 he arrived in Belgium to join the war effort. The same night he wrote off one of the squadron's motor tenders by driving it into a ditch and was given a final warning.

The next morning, flying two-seat Voisin biplane, Warneford encountered the enemy for the first time whilst flying a patrol near Ostend and Zeebrugge. He successfully harassed a German reconnaissance aircraft and over the coming weeks his determined aggressiveness resulted in him engaging in combat with any enemy aircraft he found.

Despite his reputation as a 'loose cannon' he was presented with his own machine gun-fitted Morane Saulnier monoplane fighter and given free rein to attack the enemy at will. He also flew a two-seat Nieuport biplane on anti-Zeppelin patrols and it was in this aircraft that he engaged the German airship LZ39 on May 17. With Leading Mechanic G E Meddis in the front seat operating

**Reginald Alexander John Warneford, VC (October 15, 1891 – June 17, 1915)**

the gun, the biplane raked the airship with bullets before it climbed into cloud and escaped.

Other missions resulted in serious damage to Warneford's fighter and he was eventually allotted a second, standby, machine: a parasol-winged Morane Saulnier Type L coded 3253. It would be this aeroplane that he would fly on his most famous mission.

On June 7, 1915 Warneford was part of a flight of aircraft despatched from Ghent, Belgium to find and destroy three Zeppelins that had just bombed mainland Britain and were thought to be returning to Germany.

Two Henri Farman bombers were tasked with bombing the recently

located airship sheds and both Warneford and a Lt Rose, flying a pair of Moranes, were instructed to find and destroy the Zeppelins.

Warneford had his ground crew load the aircraft with six 20lb (9kg) Hales bombs beneath the fuselage and took off from Furnes airfield near Dunkirk, France just after 1.00am.

Just minutes later he saw an airship – the LZ37 – over Ostend at 6,000ft (1,829m) and set off in pursuit. As it happened it was not one of the attackers, but he set course regardless and it took 45 minutes to catch the Zeppelin. By this time its defensive gunners were aware of Warneford's presence and began firing. He elected to climb above the airship and 20 minutes later he reached 11,000ft (3,353m). Warneford switched off the Morane's rotary engine and began a diving attack, dropping his bombs just 150ft (46m) above the LZ37.

The resulting explosion propelled the fighter onto its back and upwards – inverted – for some 200ft (61m), while the airship fell through the roof of a convent below and deposited the only survivor into a nun's (unoccupied) bed!

Back up at altitude Warneford was unable to start the Morane's engine and was eventually forced to land behind enemy lines. After 45 minutes of 'tinkering' he managed to fix a break in the fuel line and took off again. He couldn't get his bearings though so he landed in northern France and awaited daylight before scrounging some oil

**A Morane Saulnier Type L in RFC markings, similar to that flown by Reginald Warneford in 1915**

Lanoe George Hawker VC, DSO
(December 30, 1890 – November 23, 1916)

Lanoe Hawker's Bristol Scout '1611' at rest in June 1915. Note the 'rigged up' Lewis gun

from a French Army unit and returning to Furnes at 10.30am.

The following day Warneford was told he had been awarded the Victoria Cross for his amazingly brave attack and three days later a telegram announced the award; the first time a VC had been announced in such a manner.

On June 17, Warneford also received the award of Légion d'honneur from the French Army Commander in Chief, General Joffre.

Following a celebratory lunch, Warneford then travelled to the aerodrome at Buc in order to collect a Farman aircraft for delivery to the RNAS at Veurne. He made a short test flight before offering a trip to American freelance journalist. The aircraft climbed away and performed a short display for the gathered onlookers – but at 200ft (61m) the aircraft's wings folded and both men were killed as the tangled wreckage hit the ground.

The body of Reginald Warneford was brought to London and more than

## " The airship fell through a convent and deposited the only survivor into a nun's (unoccupied) bed! "

50,000 people attended his funeral at Brompton Ceremony. The wildcard, loose cannon had become a national hero.

### VC For An Ace
The third pilot to be awarded the VC was Lanoe George Hawker, who flew with 6 Sqn and eventually achieved 'ace' status with a tally of seven enemy aircraft shot down.

Hawker was born in Longparish, Hampshire on December 30, 1890 and at the age of 11 was sent to the Royal Naval College in Dartmouth. However, ill health and resultant poor grades

resulted in the Navy losing interest in the youngster and he eventually transferred to the Royal Military Academy in Woolwich before joining the Royal Engineers, as an officer cadet.

In the meantime Hawker had become fascinated with flying and after attending an air display at Bournemouth in 1910 he decided to self-fund his way to an Aviator's Certificate. His academic studies punctuated flying training at Hendon on Deperdussin monoplanes and it was March 4, 1913 before the Royal Aero Club awarded him the 435th pilot's certificate in Britain.

A subsequent request to join the Royal Flying Corps (RFC) was granted and Hawker was sent to the Central Flying School at Upavon on August 1, 1914. Training required was negligible and by October he was in France flying as a Captain with 6 Sqn; which was equipped at the time with Farman biplanes but soon reequipped with the BE.2c.

Hawker undertook various

Lanoe Hawker's 24 Sqn Airco DH.2 '5964'
*Andy Hay/www.flyingart.co.uk*

**John Aidan Liddell VC, MC**
**(August 3, 1888 – August 31, 1915)**

**Gilbert Stuart Martin Insall VC, MC**
**(May 14, 1894 – February 17, 1972)**

**Richard Bell-Davies VC, CB, DSO, AFC**
**(May 19, 1886 – February 26, 1966)**

reconnaissance missions over the autumn and winter and was wounded by ground fire at least twice.

On April 18, 1915 he was awarded the Distinguished Service Order (DSO) for a daring attack on a heavily defended Zeppelin shed and subsequently promoted to Captain of 6 Sqn's A Flight.

On June 3, the squadron received state-of-the-art Bristol Scouts and Hawker rigged his up with a Lewis gun. However, the lack of interrupter gear meant the gun could not fire through the propeller arc so needed to be mounted at an angle – resulting in the pilot needing to 'crab' whenever he wanted to shoot at the enemy!

Hawker's first flight in the modified aircraft (Scout 1609) occurred on June 7 when he shot down a German aircraft soon after getting airborne. The following day his Scout was damaged after running out of petrol and he was allocated aircraft 1611, which he similarly modified.

On July 25, Hawker was flying this

aircraft in the Passchendale area of Belgium when he encountered a German two-seater. He emptied an entire drum of ammunition before it span into the ground smoking. He then spotted a second machine and watched it dive to earth (later intelligence confirmed it had force landed behind German lines).

Next Hawker climbed the Scout to 11,000ft (3,353m) and noticed a German Albatros C.1 biplane. Attacking out of the sun he dived to within 100 yards (91m) of the German before opening fire and watching the enemy turn over and dive into the ground – pilot Oberleutnant Übelacker and observer Hauptmann Roser were both killed.

Upon his return to base Lanoe Hawker was recommended for a VC – not only for his exploits that day but in recognition of almost a year of constant operational flying. He was the first pilot to be awarded the medal for air-to-air combat.

Other victories would soon come his way and in late 1915 he was posted

back to Britain with seven victory claims (consisting of one 'captured', three 'destroyed', one 'out of control' and one 'forced to land'); making him the first British flying ace.

Back in England he was promoted to Major and placed in command of 24 Sqn; the RFC's first single-seat fighter squadron. The unit was equipped with the new Airco DH.2, which had an unsavoury reputation for spinning. However, Hawker learned the required technique to recover from this manoeuvre, taught his men, and led them to battle in France. Under his leadership 24 Sqn claimed 70 victories between February and November 1916 for the loss of just 21 pilots and 12 aircraft.

## Victim of the Red Baron
However, tragedy would strike on November 23 when Lanoe Hawker was flying DH.2 number 5964. Over Achiet, France the British ace engaged in a lengthy dogfight with an Albatros D.II

The Vickers Gunbus was a hopeless aircraft, even for its time, and with a full load of bombs its 100hp Gnome rotary engine was lucky if it could push the 'fighter' along at 60mph

The Nieuport series of scout fighters was one of the most successful of the Great War. Bell-Davies was flying a Nieuport 12 during the flight for which he received the VC

Lionel Wilmot Brabazon-Rees VC, OBE, MC, AFC, RAF
(July 31, 1884 – September 28, 1955)

Brabazon-Rees first saw action flying the cumbersome Vickers FB.5 Gunbus. On July 28, 1915 he attacked and drove down a hostile monoplane despite the main spar of his machine having been shot through and the rear spar shattered

## " He dived to within 100 yards of the German before opening fire "

flown by Lt Manfred von Richthofen – the so-called Red Baron. The German is said to have fired 900 rounds during the 30-minute battle and as his fuel ran low Hawker turned for home.

Moments later von Richthofen's guns jammed and it took a few minutes for him to rectify the situation; but all the time he remained on Hawker's tail. Finally, with the last remnants of his ammunition he fired a short burst and a single bullet struck Hawker in the back of his head, killing him instantly. His DH.2 spun into the ground and Lanoe Hawker became the 11th of the Red Baron's eventual 80 victories. He was just 25 years of age and is listed on the Arras Flying Services Memorial for airmen lost with no known grave.

### Military Cross & Victoria Cross

Captain John Aiden Liddell was the next pilot to be credited a Victoria Cross, although the quick thinking Geordie had already been awarded the Military Cross (MC) for his actions in the Army.

Born in Newcastle-upon-Tyne on August 3, 1888 and educated at Oxford University, Liddell volunteered for military duty in 1912 because, in his own words, he "did not wish to be a slacker."

In 1914, at the age of 26, he fought as a Captain with the 3rd Battalion of The Argyll and Sutherland Highlanders within the British Army and would eventually spend 43 consecutive days in the French trenches in command of a machine gun section – an effort that resulted in him being awarded the MC in January 1915.

However, earlier the previous year he had gained his civilian Royal Aero Club Pilot's Certificate (No 781) at Brooklands, Surrey and subsequently transferred to the RFC in May 1915.

Brabazon-Rees was flying an Airco DH.2 similar to this during the flight that earned him his Victoria Cross

Travelling back to France in July, Liddell reported to 7 Sqn at St Omer and began to fly operational reconnaissance missions in the Royal Aircraft Factory RE.5. His first sortie took place on July 29 and two days later he flew his second and final trip.

Flying RE.5 number 2457 with Second Lt R H Peck as observer, Liddell took off from base just before lunch to fly a reconnaissance sortie over Ostend-Bruges-Ghent, Belgium. They arrived over Bruges, Belgium at 5,000ft (1,524m) and Peck prepared his Lewis gun but, without warning, the RE.5 was suddenly fired on from above.

Peck began to return fire but suddenly the RE.5 fell onto its back and the gunner, who was not strapped in, fell from the cockpit and hung onto his gun for dear life. Unbeknown to him Liddell had been severely wounded in the attack and had now passed out.

The RE.5 plummeted around 3,000ft (914m) before Liddell finally came to

and was able to right the machine. He had been shot in the thigh and, with the bone exposed, was rapidly losing blood. The aircraft was also badly damaged: the control wheel was broken in two; the throttle damaged and the undercarriage destroyed. Liddell had little hope of returning to Allied lines but knew that if he performed an emergency landing to gain medical assistance, he and his colleague would become prisoners of war. He decided to head west towards friendly territory, scribbling a note to that effect and passing it to Peck.

In the end he managed to keep the crippled aircraft straight and level for almost 30 minutes – albeit at full power due to the broken throttle – before he reached the Belgian airfield at La Panne. He shut the engine off and glided down for a faultless landing; despite the damaged undercarriage.

He had sacrificed his own wellbeing to bring back his observer and the aircraft but despite having his leg

William Leefe-Robinson VC
(July 14, 1895 – December 31, 1918)

A souvenir postcard issued to commemorate Leefe-Robinson's successful shooting down of Schütte-Lanz SL 11 airship on September 3, 1915

Along with the Nieuport 11 and the Airco DH.2, the Royal Aircraft Factory Farman Experimental 2 (FE.2) played an instrumental role in ending the so-called 'Fokker Scourge'

amputated, Liddell died of septic poisoning a month later on August 31. By then he had been notified that he had been awarded the VC in addition to his MC.

## Living to Tell the Tale

Many of the early aerial VC recipients died in the combat for which they were recognised, but a notable exception was Gilbert Insall; the fifth pilot to receive the medal.

Gilbert Stuart Martin Insall was born in Paris, France on May 14, 1894; the son of a British dentist working in the city. He had intended to follow in his father's footsteps but the outbreak of the Great War led him to enlist in the British Army in September 1914, however in March 1915 he requested a transfer to the RFC.

Flying training began at Brooklands and he received his 'wings' after just a few days of instruction. Further tutelage in the nuances of air combat followed

Leefe-Robinson was flying a Royal Aircraft Factory BE.2c during the flight for which he was awarded the VC

and by July he had been posted back to France to fly Vickers FB.5 Gunbus two-seaters with 11 Sqn.

The Gunbus was a hopeless aircraft, even for its time, and with a full load of bombs its 100hp Gnome rotary engine was lucky if it could push the 'fighter' along at 60mph (52kts). Nonetheless Insall took this antiquated aeroplane to war and showed a keen interest in shooting down any German aircraft that

came his way.

His most notable sortie occurred on November 7, 1915 near Achiet-le-Grand, France while flying Gunbus 5074. He was joined in the cockpit by Air Mechanic T H Donald and during their patrol the pair engaged an Aviatik two-seater.

The German aircraft was forced down in a ploughed field near German lines and after seeing the crew scramble to safety, Insall descended to 500ft (152m) to drop an incendiary bomb on the aircraft. The Aviatik was destroyed but as they climbed away, heavy guns from the German trenches opened fire and the FB.5 was hit in the fuel tank.

Insall managed to land 500 yards (457m) inside Allied lines and spent the next few hours dodging around 150 enemy shells that tried to destroy the aircraft. With nightfall they used torchlight as they fixed their machine and at dawn they took off and flew back to base.

**Thomas Mottershead VC, DCM
(January 17, 1892 – January 12, 1917)**

**A 100 Sqn FE.2 readies for a night sortie on the Western Front in 1917**

The feat earned Insall the VC but he was unable to receive it in person as he and Donald were shot down again in Gunbus 5074 on December 14. This time he was wounded and captured but on August 28, 1917 – on his third attempt – he managed to escape and made his way back to British lines.

Gilbert Insall survived the war and was later awarded the Military Cross for escaping from the POW camp. In the late 1920s and 30s he served the RAF both at home and abroad and in 1927-28 he fought against the Akhwan in Southern Mesopotamia (now Iraq); receiving a 'Mention in Despatches' and the General Service Medal. He remained with the RAF as a Wing Commander throughout World War Two and finally retired in July 1945 at the age of 51. He eventually passed away peacefully at the age of 77.

Another VC winner who survived both wars was Richard Bell-Davies, the sixth man to receive the medal for services in

the air.

Born on May 19, 1886 in Kensington, London, Bell-Davies was orphaned by the age of six and was brought up by an uncle. Following his education he enlisted in the Royal Navy in April 1901 and spent more than a decade as a keen and talented seaman.

In 1910 he began paying for his own flying lessons at Hendon and received Royal Aero Club certificate number 90 in May 1911. He then made a formal application to join the RNAS as a flying officer and was accepted 18 months later.

In May 1914 Bell-Davies was sent to British Somaliland to operate against the so-called 'Mad Mullah' (religious leader Mohammed Abdullah Hassan) but the outbreak of the Great War saw him and his colleagues recalled to Europe.

In August Bell-Davies was assigned to 3 Sqn RNAS and sent to Ostend, Belgium from where he carried out a

number of raids on German submarine bases during the early days of the war; earning himself a DSO for one such mission on January 23, 1915 while flying a Farman.

During that mission Bell-Davies was injured by shrapnel and it would be some time before he returned to operational flying, but over the course of the year he would take part in some of the most significant action of the war. This included providing air cover for the ANZAC landings at Suvla and bombing air supply routes in Bulgaria.

On November 19, during a mission against Otoman-controlled forces in Bulgaria the 29-year-old Bell-Davies saw extensive action over Ferejik Junction. Flying a locally modified two-seat Nieuport 12 – coded 3172 – with the front cockpit fared over, the pilot asked the ground crew to load biplane with six 20lb (9kg) Hales bombs and launched from the Turkish island of Imbros.

**Francis Hubert 'Frank' McNamara,
VC, CB, CBE
(April 4, 1894 – November 2, 1961)**

**Frank McNamara VC (far left) with other members of 1 Sqn's C Flight, including Capt Richard Williams (third from right), and Lt Lawrence Wackett (far right), in front of a Martinsyde near the Suez Canal, Egypt in 1917**

William Avery 'Billy' Bishop, VC, CB, DSO & Bar, MC, DFC, ED
(February 8, 1894 –September 11, 1956)

A Nieuport 17, similar to that flown by 'Billy' Bishop, photographed in 1916

'Billy' Bishop's Nieuport 17 was registered B1566 and coded C-5. It also wore his trademark blue nose; the mark of an ace
Andy Hay/www.flyingart.co.uk

His flight to the target in Ferejik – just across the Turkish border in Bulgaria – went without hitch and he dropped his bombs successfully. He was just turning for home when he noticed one of 3 Sqn's Farman bombers on the ground. Flown by Flt Sub Lt Gilbert Smylie, the Farman had been struck by ground fire and its engine had failed. Smylie had made a safe landing but Bulgarian troops were advancing so he had set fire to the aircraft and was now hiding nearby.

Bell-Davies decided to attempt to land and pick up the stranded pilot before he fell into enemy hands. He began an approach to the soft marshy ground but was shocked when the Farman exploded. Smylie had noticed the incoming Nieuport and remembered his own aircraft was still carrying a live bomb; not wanting it to explode close to his comrade, he had quickly fired a pistol shot to detonate it!

Moments later Bell-Davies landed safely and Smylie clambered into the cockpit, crouching on all fours between

'Billy' Bishop was an ace and the first Canadian pilot VC recipient of the First World War. He was officially credited with 72 victories, making him the top Canadian scorer of the war

the pilot and the instrument panel.

Despite the Nieuport's notorious lack of power and the boggy ground, the aircraft finally staggered into the air and, 45 minutes later, landed back at Imbros.

Bell-Davies was awarded the VC on January 1, 1916 and Smylie received the Distinguished Service Cross (DSC).

Bell Davies remained in the RNAS and, later, Fleet Air Arm, until 1944 when he retired as a Vice Admiral. He eventually passed away in 1966 at the age of 79.

## The Welsh Ace
The first Welshman to receive the VC for valour in the air was Lionel Wilmot Brabazon Rees.

Born in Caernarfon, North Wales on July 31, 1884 Rees entered the Royal Military Academy at Woolwich, London in 1902 and was soon commissioned into the Royal Garrison Artillery and was posted to Gibraltar in 1904. Four years later he moved to Sierra Leone and was then seconded to the Southern Nigeria Regiment in May 1913.

During home leave in 1912 Rees learned to fly at his own expense and he received Aviator's Certificate number 392 in January 1913. He was seconded to the RFC in August 1914, initially as an instructor at Upavon, Wiltshire, but in early 1915 he was promoted to the

Albert Ball, VC, DSO & Two Bars, MC (August 14, 1896 – May 7, 1917)

The Austin-Ball A.F.B.1 (Austin Fighting Biplane) was a prototype built by the Austin Motor Company with design input from Albert Ball. Although trials showed it to be a fine aeroplane the A.F.B.1 did not go into production, as both Austin's production capacity and its Hispano-Suiza engine were required for the SE5a

rank of Captain and took command of the newly formed 11 Sqn at Netheravon, Wiltshire.

In July Rees took the squadron to France where he and his colleagues first saw action flying the cumbersome Vickers FB.5 Gunbus. On July 28, he attacked and drove down a hostile monoplane despite the main spar of his machine having been shot through and the rear spar shattered. Other missions followed and on August 31 he fought a German LVG biplane bomber for 45 minutes before expending his ammunition. He then returned for more ammunition and went out to the attack again, finally downing the enemy machine. These other missions earned Rees the Military Cross on September 21, 1915.

Late in the year he returned to Britain to command of the Central Flying School Flight at Upavon but in June 1916 he returned to France; this time in charge of the newly formed 32 Sqn flying the newly arrived Airco DH.2 'pusher'.

During the opening hours of the Somme Offensive, Rees – flying DH.2 6015 – took off from Treizennes, near

## "Insall spent the next few hours dodging 150 enemy shells"

Aire at 5.55am and attempted to join forces with other British aeroplanes to counter German fighters and bombers threatening the ground forces. However, Rees soon became separated from his colleagues and, flying alone near Double Crassieurs, he sighted a formation of bombers. Initially Rees misidentified them as British aeroplanes but upon getting closer realised his error and opened fire. Within moments one of the bombers began to spiral away to safety so Rees lined up on the next. By now other German aircraft were attacking the plucky Welshman but he pressed on with his own mission and soon a second bomber was smoking and turning for home.

Next, Rees turned his sights towards five other bombers that had recently appeared; diving head-on towards them while firing an entire drum of

ammunition. He then turned and was attacking the lead aircraft when he felt a sharp pain in his leg – he'd been hit.

Although unable to use the rudder bar, Rees pressed on with the attack, causing significant damage before landing back at base at 6.50am.

He was hospitalised for several weeks after the mission, and retained a limp for the rest of his life, but on August 5 he learned that the sortie had earned him the VC.

Although he remained in the RFC and subsequent RAF until 1931 (and was called up again between 1939 and 1941) Rees would never fly again operationally. However, he finished the war as an Ace with eight confirmed aerial victories, comprising one enemy aircraft 'captured', one 'destroyed', one 'forced to land' and five 'driven down'.

In 1918, he was also awarded the Air Force Cross (AFC) for services to flight training and, interestingly, while flying from Cairo to Baghdad in the 1920s, he took some of the earliest archaeological aerial photographs of sites in eastern Transjordan (now Jordan). He is therefore considered a pioneer of aerial archaeology.

Left: Albert Ball switched between the capable Nieuport 17 and not-so-capable BE.2; an example of the latter seen here Right: In early 1917 Abert Ball was posted as a flight commander with 56 Sqn and while the unit flew the Royal Aircraft Factory SE5a, Ball was allowed to retain his personal Nieuport 17 for solo missions, providing he flew the SE5a with the rest of the squadron

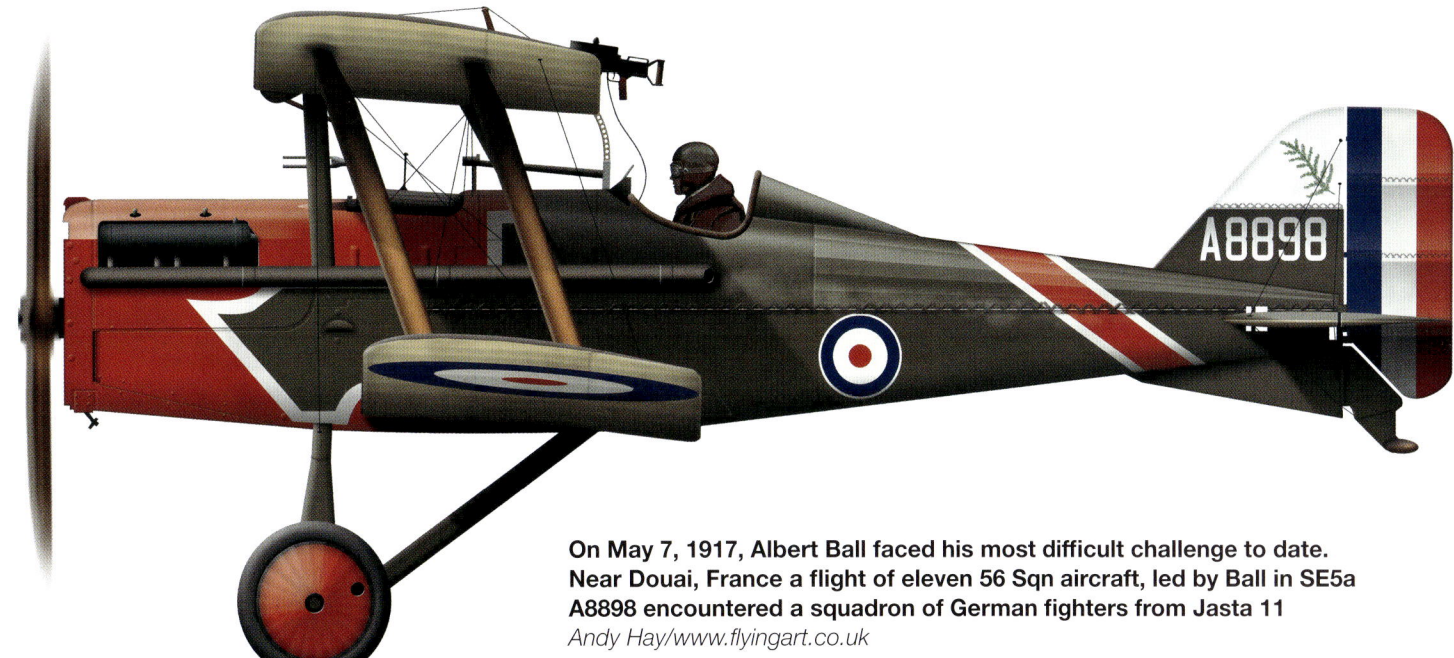

On May 7, 1917, Albert Ball faced his most difficult challenge to date. Near Douai, France a flight of eleven 56 Sqn aircraft, led by Ball in SE5a A8898 encountered a squadron of German fighters from Jasta 11

*Andy Hay/www.flyingart.co.uk*

Group Captain Lionel Wilmot Brabazon Rees VC, OBE, MC, AFC, RAF (rtd) passed away peacefully in the Bahamas on September 28, 1955 at the age of 71.

## Gallantry Over 'Blighty'

Of all 1,358 VCs ever awarded only six have been earned by men fighting in (or over) the mainland UK. The first recipient was William Leefe-Robinson, the eighth aviator to receive the medal.

William Leefe-Robinson was born in Coorg, India on July 14, 1895. The youngest of seven, he attended Bishop Cotton Boys' School in Bangalore before being sent to Britain for advanced education.

In August 1914 he entered the Royal Military College at Sandhurst and after transferring to the RFC he went to France the following March as an observer. Serving with 4 Sqn at St Omer he was injured in the arm on May 9, 1915 while flying over Lille in a BE.2c flown by Maj Longcroft and was invalided back to Britain.

During his time back in back in Britain Leefe-Robinson applied for pilot training and after acceptance was sent to Farnborough, Hampshire on June 29. He soloed on July 18 and qualified ten days later before being sent to Upavon for more training. His 'wings' were granted on September 15 but it would be February the following year before he was allocated to an operational unit: the night-fighting 39 (Home Defence) Sqn at Hornchurch, Kent.

Flying BE.2c aircraft as makeshift night fighters to defend against German airships was far from ideal; there were no radios, oxygen, heating or parachutes and it could take an hour or more for the woefully underpowered aircraft to reach the 10,000ft (3,048m) operating altitude favoured by the airships.

Lt Leefe-Robinson saw his first airship on the night of April 25/26 but as soon as he opened fire the German crew jettisoned ballast and climbed out of his reach. This frustrating pattern continued over the coming months until the night of September 2/3.

Shortly after take-off at 11.08pm Leefe-Robinson, flying BE.2c 2693, had spotted a dirigible but it soon disappeared in cloud and it was several hours before he saw another at 1.10am. By then it was at 11,500ft (3,505m) and, slowly, Leefe-Robinson closed to within 500ft (152m) from below. However, before he could fire, the airship – thought to be Zeppelin LZ98 – slipped into cloud and escaped. Then, shortly after 2.00am, Schütte-Lanz SL 11 – a wooden framed airship that was for many years misidentified as a 'Zeppelin' came into sight over Cuffley, Hertfordshire, slightly below Leefe-Robinson's BE.2c. The SL 11 was 571ft (174m) long and, having been launched on August 1, was only on its second mission. Its captain that night was Commander Hauptmann Wilhelm

**Alan Arnett McLeod VC
(April 20, 1899 – November 6, 1918)**

Schramm – who ironically had been born just a few miles from Cuffley when his father was working at the Siemens factory.

Leefe Robinson began a swift descent and slipped into position below the airship and, without Schramm or his colleagues realising he was there, he opened fire with a stream of incendiary bullets. His first drum of ammunition failed to damage the SL 11 and the second drum was equally ineffective, but the third (and final) batch of bullets started a small fire in the rear of the vessel. Within seconds the flames had spread and the SL 11 fell to earth behind the Plough Inn in Cuffley. Schramm and his 15-man crew were killed.

It was the first German airship downed over Britain and for his remarkable feat William Leefe-Robinson was awarded the VC on September 5, 1916. He also achieved celebrity status and grateful Londoners donated £4,300 in prize money (more than £400,000 in today's money) to the plucky pilot.

His action marked a turning point in the war against the airship menace, and caused the German airship bombing campaign to falter. In the three months afterwards five more airships were shot down, using the combat techniques he had proven.

Following a crash on September 16, the famous pilot was grounded (he was considered too valuable by now) but after much pleading the RFC finally allowed Leefe Robinson to return to active service in April 1917. He then joined 48 Sqn in France flying the Bristol F.2 Fighter but on April 5 he was shot down by Vizefeldwebel Sebastian Festner and was wounded and captured.

He constantly tried to escape but was not repatriated until December 1918, by which time his health was in rapid decline. Over Christmas he contracted Spanish flu and died on New Year's Eve.

**Alan Jerrard VC**
**(December 3, 1897 – May 14, 1968)**

Jerrard's was assigned to 19 Sqn and joined the squadron at Liettres, France in July 1916 to fly Spad S.VII single-seaters similar to this airframe

## Fighting in a 'Fee'

Along with the Nieuport 11 and the Airco DH.2, the Royal Aircraft Factory FE.2 (Farman Experimental 2) played an instrumental role in ending the so-called 'Fokker Scourge' that had seen the German Air Service establish a measure of air superiority on the Western Front from the late summer of 1915 to the following spring. However, just one 'Fee' pilot was awarded the VC for his actions.

Thomas Mottershead was born in Widnes, Lancashire on January 17, 1892 and after leaving school he became an apprentice fitter and turner and was working as a garage mechanic in Andover, Hampshire when war broke out in 1914. The 21–year-old was already married and a son followed shortly after he enlisted in the RFC.

He was initially posted to Central Flying School at Upavon and spent 18

## " It was the first German airship downed over Britain "

months maintaining the school's aircraft before the urge to fly got the better of him and he applied to become a pilot in May 1916.

Mottershead quickly proved himself to be an excellent aviator and qualified within a month before spending a short period as a flying instructor. However, on July 5 he was sent to France where he joined 25 Sqn at Auchel to fly the FE.2.

One of his first operations was a low-level bombing raid on a German anti-aircraft battery, which he successfully disabled. Then, on September 22, he bombed the railway station at Samain, destroying an ammunition train and damaging another.

Moments later, while climbing away from the target, the aircraft was attacked by a Fokker scout but Mottershead's skilful flying enabled his gunner, Second Lt Street, to shoot down the enemy aircraft. For this, and his track record to date, Mottershead was awarded the Distinguished Conduct Medal and promoted to the rank of Flight Sergeant.

Soon afterwards the young pilot transferred to 20 Sqn at Clairmarais. On January 7, 1917 Flt Sgt Mottershead and his observer Lt W E Gower took off in FE.2d A39 just before noon and routed towards Ploegsteert Wood in Belgium where they had been tasked with flying a patrol in company with another 'Fee' crew.

Arriving over the area at 10,000ft (3,048m) they were soon engaged in combat by a pair of Albatros D.III fighters from Jasta 8. Gower managed to hit one of the German aircraft, which

The Sopwith Camel was introduced on the Western Front in 1917 and was a development of the earlier Sopwith Pup. In total, Camel pilots have been credited with the shooting down of 1,294 enemy aircraft, more than any other Allied fighter of the conflict

Jerrard joined 66 Sqn in Italy where he flew Sopwith Camels, similar to these, between February 27 and March 21, 1917, scoring four aerial victories against Austro-Hungarian forces

span into the ground, but seconds later the other aircraft – flown by German ace Vizefeldwebel Göttsch – turned onto Mottershead's tail and fired at almost point blank range.

The FE.2d's fuel tank was pierced and the aircraft was quickly enveloped in flames. Gower was able to subdue the fire with a handheld fire extinguisher but Mottershead was in serious trouble. His flying suit was alight and as the aircraft descended, ground troops could clearly see Gower trying to put out the pilot's flaming clothes with his bare hands.

At this point it would have been possible to make a controlled forced-landing but Mottershead was determined to reach Allied lines. Finally, he deemed it safe to land, found a suitable field, flew a conventional circuit and turned the burning FE.2 into wind. Despite lowering the aircraft as gently

as he could the damaged undercarriage collapsed immediately. Gower was thrown clear but Mottershead was pinned in the burning fuselage and it took several minutes for his observer and members of a nearby Army unit to extricate him from the wreckage. He was badly burned, but alive, and was sent for medical attention. Five days later 24-year-old Thomas Mottershead passed away on January 12. Like so many after him he had sacrificed his own life for that of his crewmate. Exactly a month later it was announced that he would be awarded the VC and Gower would receive the MC for his role in the extraordinary event. Mottershead's VC – the only one ever awarded to a non-commissioned RFC officer during the Great War – was presented to his widow by King George V in a ceremony in Hyde Park, London on June 2, 1917.

## Australia's First

The first and only Australian aviator to receive the VC during the Great War was Frank McNamara, who would later go on to become an Air Vice Marshal and a senior commander in the Royal Australian Air Force (RAAF).

Francis Hubert (Frank) McNamara was born in Victoria, Australia on April 4, 1894 and worked as a teacher prior to joining the war effort in 1915 and being selected for pilot training.

Sent to Point Cook Air Base to learn to fly on Bristol Boxkites, McNamara joined the Australian Flying Corps' 1 Sqn in 1916. The unit was posted to Egypt to work alongside the RFC but upon arrival McNamara and most of his colleagues were sent on to Britain for additional 'operational flying training.' McNamara arrived at Filton, Somerset on May 16 and passed through various units

Alan Jerrard was flying Camel B5648 – coded E – in formation with Peter Carpenter in Camel B7387 and Harold Ross Eycott-Martin in B7283 during the flight that earned him the VC
*Andy Hay/www.flyingart.co.uk*

**Alan Jerrard pictured with his Spad S.VII during the war**

before returning to Egypt on August 24 and finally re-joining his squadron, which was now equipped with a mix of obsolete BE.2cs, BE.2es and Martinsyde G.100 Scouts.

His stay with the unit was brief however as he contracted Orchitus and was hospitalised for a month before spending a period as a flying instructor. It was therefore December 22, 1916 before McNamara flew his first combat mission (in BE.2c 4475).

His most notable sortie occurred on March 20, 1917 when, flying Martinsyde 7486, McNamara formed part of a four-ship attacking a German military

railway near Tel al Hesi. The formation consisted of two BE.2cs (flown by Capt David Rutherford and Lt Roy 'Peter' Drummand) and two Martinsydes (flown by McNamara and Lt Alf Ellis), each armed with six 4.5in Howitzer shells that had been modified into bombs and fitted with 40-second delay fuses.

After departing their base at El Arish all four aircraft dropped their weapons on the rail tracks. However, one of McNamara's bombs exploded prematurely as it was leaving the aircraft; fragments of shell casing tore into the fabric wings and one jagged piece of metal lodged itself in the pilot's right buttock.

Shortly afterwards Ellis sighted a German aircraft but before he could join the fight McNamara spotted one of the BE.2c's on the ground and Turkish cavalry charging towards the aircraft. Allied airmen had been hacked to death by enemy troops in similar situations.

The stricken aircraft was Rutherford's (4479) and without hesitation McNamara landed on the rough ground next to his friend, who was attempting to set fire to his machine.

As there was nowhere for Rutherford to sit in the single-seat Martinsyde, the downed pilot jumped onto McNamara's wing and held the struts. The

**James Thomas Byford McCudden, VC, DSO & Bar, MC & Bar, MM (March 18, 1895 – July 9, 1918)**

**The cockpit of an SE5a, similar to that flown by various VC holders including James McCudden**

James McCudden poses for the camera in 1918

combination of his painful wound and the overloading of the aircraft caused the Australian to crash while attempting to take-off but luckily neither pilot was injured in the 'prang.' The two men then set fire to the BE.2c and dashed back to Rutherford's BE.2c.

Rutherford repaired the engine while McNamara used his revolver against the attacking cavalry, who were now firing on them. Eventually the two managed to take-off and although he was in immense pain and close to blacking out from lack of blood McNamara flew the damaged aircraft 70 miles (110km) back to El Arish – a flight lasting 1 hour and 20 minutes.

Shortly after landing the brave Aussie lost consciousness but a contemporary news report declared that he was "soon sitting up, eating chicken and drinking champagne".

On March 26 Frank McNamara was recommended for the Victoria Cross by Brigadier General Geoffrey Salmond, General Officer Commanding Middle East Brigade, RFC and the decoration was announced on June 8, 1917.

As a result of his leg injury McNamara never flew operationally again but he served as a flying instructor and progressed through the ranks of the post war RAAF. In 1942 he was appointed AOC British Forces Aden but retired from the military in 1946. Frank McNamara continued to live in England after the war and eventually passed away of heart failure on November 2, 1961 at the age of 67.

## " Without hesitation McNamara landed next to his friend "

### Canada's Greatest Ace

The eleventh pilot awarded the VC during the Great War also happened to the Canada's greatest flying ace.

William Avery 'Billy' Bishop, who was officially credited with 72 victories, traced his history back to the small town of Owen Sound in Ontario. He was a notorious rebel, shunning convention and team sports as a child and favouring solitary pastimes. He was also known to be a fighter who was not afraid of defending himself (and others) against bullies.

In 1911 Bishop entered the Royal Military College of Canada (RMC) in Kingston, Ontario and despite failing his first year he eventually completed three years as a cadet before the Great War broke out in 1914.

At this point he joined a cavalry regiment and sailed for Europe in June 1915. He lasted just a month before he requested a transfer to the RFC, but with no pilot vacancies he was forced to settle for an observer role. Following training at Netheravon, Wiltshire he was attached to 21 Sqn and sent to France on January 1, 1916 to fly in the back of the then state-of-the-art Royal Aircraft Factory RE.5 aircraft.

A series of incidents and prangs

resulted in Bishop being injured on a number of occasions and his final mission as an observer occurred on May 2, 1916. He then returned to England to recuperate from an injured knee and it would be September before he was fit for duty again. However, he had been approved for pilot training and in November he reported to Upavon for instruction.

'Billy' Bishop was not a natural pilot and it took him a while to get the hang of landing – in fact he continued to suffer the occasional bumpy arrival throughout his career – but he eventually gained his wings and was briefly allocated to 37 (Home Defence) Sqn at Hornchurch to fly night missions. He soon returned to France though, where he joined 60 Sqn flying Nieuport 17 Scouts.

On March 25, 1917 he scored his first victory when he shot down an Albatros D.III near St Leger, but moments later his engine cut and he was forced to land between shell holes on mudflats. Perhaps this was not the ending he hoped for his first victorious sortie but it marked the beginning of a remarkable career.

In addition to the usual patrols with his squadron mates, Bishop soon began flying unofficial 'lone-wolf' missions across enemy lines and on April 8 he celebrated his fifth victory by painting the nose of his personal Nieuport 17 (B1566) blue; the mark of an ace.

Bishop claimed 12 aircraft in April alone, winning the Military Cross and a promotion to Captain for his

Ferdinand Maurice Felix 'Freddy' West, VC, CBE, MC (January 19, 1896 – July 8, 1988)

'Freddy' West earned his VC flying the lumbering Armstrong Whitworth FK.8

participation at the Battle of Vimy Ridge. The following month he won the Distinguished Service Order (DSO) for shooting down two aircraft while being attacked by four others and on June 2 he flew his most notorious mission.

After getting lost in low cloud one morning Bishop suddenly discovered he was over a German-held airfield behind enemy lines. He dropped to 200ft (61m) and began to strafe the aircraft that were being prepared for the day's flying. Some of the German pilots attempted to get airborne but by the end of the confrontation Bishop had claimed three aircraft that were shot down while taking off to attack him and he also claimed to have destroyed several more on the ground. Although some questioned the validity of his claim Bishop was nominated for a VC and although there were no witnesses to his attack the medal was awarded on August 9.

By this time 60 Sqn had traded its Nieuports in for faster and more powerful Royal Aircraft Factory SE5s and shortly after the award of his VC Bishop passed the late Albert Ball [see below] in victories to temporarily become the highest scoring RFC ace.

After a period of home leave in Canada, Bishop returned to the war in May 1918, this time in command of the SE5a-equipped 85 Sqn. By the end of the war, he had claimed some 72 air victories – although official RCAF historians have since suggested the actual total was far lower. Regardless of the exact numbers 'Billy' Bishop was one of the greatest fighter pilots of his generation and a worthy winner of the VC.

During World War Two Bishop became instrumental in setting up and promoting the British Commonwealth Air Training Plan, which trained over 167,000 airmen in Canada. He died in

his sleep on September 11, 1956, at the age of 62, while wintering in Palm Beach, Florida.

## Nottingham's Finest

The twelfth pilot to receive the Victoria Cross was Albert Ball. Born in the Lenton area of Nottingham on August 14, 1896, Ball spent his formative years in the city and joined the Sherwood Foresters at the outbreak of the Great War as a commissioned second lieutenant.

However, with no sign of being sent to a battlefront, Ball requested a transfer to the RFC and paid for his own flight training at Hendon. He qualified for his Aviator's Certificate (No 1898) on October 15, 1915 and following additional training by the military he gained his RFC wings on January 26 of the following year. Three days later he was officially accepted by the RFC and after a brief period instructing with 22 Sqn at Gosport, Hampshire he was allocated to 13 Sqn in Marieux, France on February 18 to fly the BE.2c in the reconnaissance role.

## " He destroyed three Roland C.IIs in a single sortie "

On May 7 Ball transferred to 11 Sqn to fly Bristol Scout fighters and on May 16 he scored his first aerial victory, driving down a German reconnaissance aircraft. He then switched to Nieuports, bringing down two LVGs on 29 May and a Fokker Eindecker on June 1. On 25 June Ball became a balloon buster and an ace by destroying an observation balloon with phosphorus bombs.

Following a request for a few days off, Ball was dismayed to be temporarily reassigned to aerial reconnaissance

duty with 8 Sqn flying BE.2s for a month between July 18 and August 14. It was during this time that he flew a French espionage agent across enemy lines, dodging an attack by three German fighters and anti-aircraft fire and landing in a deserted field. This, combined with his track record to date, earned the 19-year-old pilot the Military Cross.

On July 22, 1916 he destroyed three Roland C.IIs in a single one sortie; the first RFC pilot to do so. Later that day he fought 14 Germans some 15 miles (24 km) behind their lines.

The talented aviator was awarded the Distinguished Service Order (DSO) and bar simultaneously on September 26, 1916. The first award was "for conspicuous gallantry and skill" when he took on two enemy formations. The bar was also "for conspicuous skill and gallantry" when he attacked four enemy aircraft in formation and then, on another occasion, 12 enemy machines. A second bar to the DSO, for taking on three enemy aircraft and shooting one down, followed on November 25, making him the first three-time recipient of the award and a national hero.

In early 1917 Ball was posted as a flight commander with 56 Sqn and while the unit flew the Royal Aircraft Factory SE5a, Ball was allowed to retain his personal Nieuport 17 (B1522) for solo missions, providing he flew the SE5A with the rest of the squadron. Yet more victories followed and he frequently shot down multiple aircraft per sortie.

Then, on the evening of May 7, Ball faced his most difficult challenge to date. Near Douai, France a flight of eleven 56 Sqn aircraft, led by Ball in SE5a A8898 encountered a squadron of German fighters from Jasta 11. A fierce dogfight ensued and Ball was last seen pursuing a red Albatros D.III flown by the Red Baron's younger brother, Lothar von Richthofen. Both aircraft entered a thundercloud and the Albatros later landed with a punctured fuel tank but Ball was not seen alive again.

German witnesses claim to have seen his SE5a appear from the bottom of the cloud a few moments later, inverted and trailing smoke. The aircraft crashed and Ball was dead when the Germans arrived at the scene. Witnesses agreed that the crashed aircraft had suffered no battle damage and no bullet wounds were found on Ball's body. A doctor later diagnosed a broken back and a crushed chest, along with fractured limbs, as the cause of death. It is likely he became disorientated in the cloud and was unable to recover to level flight when he emerged out of the bottom of the storm. At the time of his death in May 1917, twenty-year-old Albert Ball was Britain's leading ace, with 44 victories and he remained the nation's fourth-highest scorer behind Edward 'Mick' Mannock, James McCudden, and George McElroy. He was buried with full military honours by the Germans shortly after the accident. The British government awarded him the VC on June 8.

## To Battle in the 'Big Ack'

The thirteenth aviator to be awarded the VC was another Canadian, who received the medal for valour whilst flying the Armstrong Whitworth FK.8 – a type known as the 'Big Ack' to its crews – in the army co-operation role.

Alan Arnett McLeod was born on April 20, 1899 in Stonewall, Manitoba and enrolled in the Territorial Army at age 14. When the War started McLeod was sent home for being under age. He tried to enlist on several occasions but had to wait until he turned 18 before he was accepted by the RFC.

Flying instruction began on June 4,

**William George 'Billy' Barker, VC, DSO & Bar, MC & Two Bars (November 3, 1894 – March 12, 1930)**

1917 and McLeod received his 'wings' on July 31. The following month he was shipped to Britain with just 50 hours in his logbook. By August 20 he was in France and posted to 82 Sqn flying FK.8s, but when his commanding officer discovered McLeod was still just 18 he sent him back to Britain to fly home defence missions.

It would be some months before the youngster – by now nicknamed 'babe' – was finally approved to fly operational missions in France and he arrived at 2 Sqn at Hesdigneul on November 29.

Operating in army co-operation missions in a big lumbering biplane was far from exciting but McLeod would routinely strafe targets of opportunity whenever possible to liven up his days. On December 19 he took this one stage further and used the cumbersome aircraft to launch an attack on eight Albatros fighters! The Germans were taken by surprise and scattered, but not

before McLeod's observer (Lt Comber) had managed to shoot down one of them. The duo also claimed a Fokker Dr.I triplane as destroyed the following month and on January 14 they brought down an observation balloon near Beauvin. McLeod was mentioned in dispatches for this exploit.

However, Alan McLeod's greatest success would come on March 27, 1918 when he and observer Lt Arthur Hammond flew FK.8 B5773 in another attack on a German triplane. No sooner had the pair downed the enemy than they were 'bounced' by eight more Dr.Is from the famous 'Richthofen Circus' of Jasta 10.

Almost immediately Hammond downed one of the aggressors with a burst of machine gun fire but German ace Hans Kirchstein pulled up under the FK.8 and riddled the bomber with bullets, injuring Hammond twice. A coordinated attack by a third Dr.I left McLeod with a bullet in one leg but this made him only more determined to continue the fight. He turned the FK.8 towards the nearest German and seconds later the triplane exploded.

Kirchstein came back for another attempt at downing the RFC aircraft and this time his bullets found the FK.8's fuel tank. The aircraft immediately burst into flames and quickly the wooden floor burned through. Next, the instrument panel started to smoulder and then McLeod's flying boots caught alight.

Although most of the surviving Fokkers now turned away, one was determined to see the FK.8's ultimate demise. However, the pilot was to pay for his curiosity when Hammond – by now badly burned and severely injured – managed to loose off a final burst of gunfire that downed his third Dr.I of the day.

**On April 9, 1917 'Billy' Barker flew an R.E.8, similar to this, with his observer Lt Goodfellow to help Australian gunners range their artillery against a German assault - a mission that earned him a 'Bar' to his MC**

‘Billy’ Barker VC with a captured Fokker D.VII aircraft at Hounslow Aerodrome after the war

▶ ‘Billy’ Barker was keen to return to flying and was offered a job with a scout unit in 1917. He was given the choice of flying SE5as with 56 Sqn or Sopwith Camels with 28 Sqn and chose the latter. He is seen here with his personal aircraft at Droglandt, near Cambrai

The RFC aircraft eventually crashed in No Man's Land and although he was badly wounded and in shock, McLeod pulled the now unconscious Hammond from the wreckage and dragged him to the Allied lines before collapsing from exhaustion.

Alan McLeod was wounded three times in the side and Arthur Hammond was wounded six times. Hammond lost a leg but was awarded a bar for his Military Cross. McLeod was recommended for a DSO but was awarded the VC on May 1, 1918. He was returned to Canada to recuperate but died from Spanish Influenza shortly thereafter. He was only five months away from celebrating his 20th birthday.

## Mastering the Camel

The Sopwith Camel, which debuted above the battlefield in June 1917, was difficult to handle but provided

a high level of manoeuvrability to an experienced pilot. This alone made it a highly successful fighter and in total 1,294 enemy aircraft fell to the guns of the Camel – more than any other Allied fighter of the conflict. It is therefore strange than just a single Camel pilot received the Victoria Cross. That man was Alan Jerrard.

Alan was born in Lewisham, London on December 3, 1897 but moved to Sutton Coldfield, Warwickshire as a boy. At the end of his studies at Birmingham University Alan was commissioned as a Second Lieutenant with the South Staffordshire Regiment of the British

Army in January 1916 but after a few months in the trenches he applied for a transfer to the Royal Flying Corps where he trained as a fighter pilot.

Jerrard's first operational unit was 59 Sqn, which was preparing to fly to France, but ill health meant he was unable to join his colleagues and he was eventually reassigned to 19 Sqn. He joined the squadron at Liettres, France in July 1916 to fly Spad S.VII single-seaters and performed his first operational mission on July 29. He got lost that day and had to land back alone but on his second mission, on August 5, he had more success.

The Sopwith 7F.1 Snipe was designed as a replacement for the earlier Pup and Camel and came into squadron service a few weeks before the end of the conflict, in late 1918. It was not a fast aircraft by the standards of its time, but it boasted a good climb rate and excellent manoeuvrability

Once again, Jerrard got lost in bad weather but this time he stumbled across a German supply convoy and strafed several vehicles, causing significant damage. He then climbed up through the cloud to 10,000ft (3,048m) where his engine quit and he had to glide back down before attempting an emergency landing. He broke his nose and jaw in the ensuing crash and he was sent back to Britain for a 'refresher' course.

Afterwards, Jerrard joined 66 Sqn in Italy where he flew Sopwith Camels between February 27 and March 21, 1917, scoring four aerial victories against Austro-Hungarian forces.

On March 30 Lt Jerrard was aloft again on an offensive patrol, this time near Mansuè, Italy. He was flying Camel B5648 – coded E – in formation with Peter Carpenter in Camel B7387 and Harold Ross Eycott-Martin in B7283.

Poor weather had delayed their departure and Jerrard was so convinced that he would not be flying that day that he simply pulled his flying suit over his pyjamas as he waited for the scramble call. But they did get airborne and Jerrard quickly shot down the first of five German aircraft claimed that day. Then, flying at just 50ft (15m), he attacked an aerodrome where 19 machines were either landing or attempting to take-off.

Jerrard destroyed one of these aircraft but quickly came under attack. Undeterred he saw that his colleagues were also in danger and went to assist – destroying a third enemy machine in the process. Jerrard then continued his attacks before finally retreating (with five

## "He simply pulled his flying suit over his pyjamas"

Albatros D.IIIs in pursuit) on the stern orders of the patrol leader.

Soon the other pilots noted that Jerrard was flying "very weakly as though wounded" but he was still seen to turn repeatedly to single-handedly attack the pursuing machines, until he was eventually overwhelmed by numbers and driven to the ground 4 miles (6.5km) from Mansuè Aerodrome.

He survived the impact and was held as a prisoner of war in Salzburg by the Austrians until the end of 1918.

Alan Jerrard elected to stay in the RAF after the war and on April 5, 1919 he received his Victoria Cross from King George V at Buckingham Palace. Lt Jerrard had greatly distinguished himself on four previous occasions, within a period of just 23 days, in destroying enemy machines, displaying bravery and ability of the very highest order. He was a very worthy recipient of the medal, which he carried with pride until he passed away at the age of 70 on May 14, 1968.

## From Humble Roots

While some of the aircrew who won the VC were from privileged backgrounds, many were from humble middle or lower class roots. These included the pilot who not only won the VC but went on to be among the most highly decorated airmen in British military history.

James Thomas Byford 'Jimmy' McCudden was born in Gillingham, Kent on March 28, 1895 to a middle class family and following his education he joined the Royal Engineers in 1910.

However, the McCudden family had often taken their children to see the pioneer aviators flying on the Isle of Sheppey and young 'Jimmy' held a desire to become a pilot himself. Now he saw the war in Europe as a way of fulfilling his dream and he soon applied for a transfer to the RFC.

He initially joined the RFC as a mechanic in May 1913 and was despatched to Farnborough for training. However, his time at the base did not get off to a good start when he was instructed to familiarise himself with the Caudron biplane parked in a hangar. He turned the propeller and the engine sprung to life before the aircraft accelerated out of the hangar and collided with Farman MF.11 and his commanding officer's car!

In June 1913, McCudden was posted to 3 Sqn and a year later was promoted to Air Mechanic First Class in readiness to travel to France with the unit. McCudden soon began to fly as an observer, although he opted to take along a rifle as the two-seat Morane Saulnier parasol winged monoplanes carried no fixed armament.

By the end of 1914 he had been promoted to the rank of Corporal and by April 1915 he was a Sergeant in charge of all the unit's engines. McCudden's delight at gaining the promotion was cut short however when news arrived that his brother William had been

Barker was allocated Snipe E8102 for his two week 'tour' of France in 1918
*Andy Hay/www.flyingart.co.uk*

killed in an air crash while flying a Blériot. McCudden still made a formal application to become a pilot but it was rejected on the grounds his reputation as a mechanic had spread since due to the record-low number of engine failures since he'd taken over.

Nonetheless he continued to fly as an observer and was often paired with the unit's new commanding officer, Edgar Ludlow-Hewitt, who had taken over on November 20. The following January McCudden was awarded the Croix de Guerre for gallantry and the medal brought him to the attention of high-ranking RFC officers who ordered him home to England 24 hours later to begin pilot training!

In May 1916 McCudden became the 107th non-commissioned officer to qualify as a pilot. In fact he was so good that he was 'creamed off' to work as an instructor after flying just nine solo hours himself.

Finally, on July 8 he was allocated to 20 Sqn to begin operational flying. Equipped with Royal Aircraft Factory FE.2s at Clairmarais, the unit was active during the Battle of the Somme and McCudden's first sortie over the trenches took place on July 10. He stayed with 20 Sqn until August 2 and saw extensive flying, although he had yet to score a victory.

His next attachment was to 29 Sqn flying Airco DH.2 scouts and on September 6 he shot down his first enemy aircraft – an all-white Albatros B.II.

McCudden's next victory was on January 26, 1917 and from that point

forward the 'kills' came thick and fast. On February 16 McCudden was awarded the Military Cross for his fifth victory.

His war then progressed with alternating tours as an instructor and operational pilot. Victories came in DH.2s and Sopwith Pups but 52 of his eventual 57 kills were achieved while flying with 56 Sqn in his personal SE5a (B4863 coded 'G').

In mid-March 1918 James McCudden returned to the UK again for some home leave and it was during this time that he learned that the King had bestowed the honour of a Victoria Cross upon him.

He now had the VC, DSO & Bar, MC & Bar and a Military Medal to his name but he stayed in England until July when he was given command of 60 Sqn of the fledgling RAF (as the RFC had now been renamed).

On July 9 he picked up his new SE5a (C1126), had breakfast with his fiancé and set off for Boffles airfield in France, where 60 Sqn was to be based. Poor weather meant he had difficulty finding his destination and he landed to ask directions from RAF personnel based at Auxi-le-Château. With his map marked with the relevant information McCudden took off again, performed a tight turn for the onlookers and plummeted into the ground. His skull was fractured and he died later that evening.

Despite enjoying such a varied and successful career it must be remembered that Major James McCudden was aged just 23 at the time of his tragic demise.

## VC 'and' a CBE

The sixteenth flyer to receive the VC, Ferdinand Maurice Felix 'Freddy' West was born in Paddington, London on January 19, 1896 as the only son of a British Army officer and the grandson of the Admiral of the Fleet. His father was killed during the Second Boer War in 1902 but when war broke out in Germany 'Freddy' didn't hesitate in joining up.

His initial service saw him working as a Private in the Royal Army Medical Corps in 1914 and a year later he was commissioned and joined the Royal Munster Fusiliers. West arrived in France in November 1915 and spent the next four months knee deep in mud in the trenches.

In March 1916 he managed to 'scrounge' a flight in a 3 Sqn aeroplane and immediately requested a transfer to the RFC. Accepted as a trainee observer, he was shipped to Brooklands, Surrey for instruction and by the end of April he was back in France and attached to 3 Sqn flying operational sorties in Morane Saulnier parasol winged monoplanes.

West took any opportunity to fly as an observer, so as to boost his logbook to make him more desirable to the promotion board. By the end of July 1917 he had amassed more than 100 hours and was accepted for a pilot training course.

West made his first solo flight on November 15 and by Christmas he had accumulated 60 solo hours. On January 4, 1918 he was posted back to France and joined 8 Sqn at Amiens under the command of Maj Trafford Leigh-Mallory.

With 8 Sqn West was destined to fly army co-operation sorties in the Armstrong Whitworth FK.8 and he soon settled into squadron life, forming a regular partnership with observer Lt John Haslam.

The missions were varied and dangerous and on May 1 both West and Haslam received the Military Cross for their on-going bravery and fortitude. On June 18 the pair's big General Purpose biplane was attacked by four Pfalz D.III scouts but West managed to shoot one of the much more agile German fighters and evade the other three. The following day the duo were 'bounced' by a flight of Fokker D.VIIs and when West dropped to 200ft (61m) to evade the fighters he found himself in the midst of a barrage balloon network and had to skilfully fly around the steel cables to make his escape. The action earned him a promotion to Captain and he was made a flight commander.

In August 1918 West and Haslam were heavily involved in supporting the infantry and tanks as the Allies swept forward into German territory. On August 10 the duo flew FK.8 C8594 from the base in support of tanks advancing on nearby Roye. It was a misty day but suddenly a gap appeared near Hombleux and 'Freddy' West quickly noticed a large concentration of German troops and vehicles. Breaking clear of cloud he descended to observe the enemy formation but was met with a

**Andrew Frederick Weatherby Beauchamp-Proctor, VC, DSO, MC & Bar, DFC (September 4, 1894 – June 21, 1921)**

curtain of anti-aircraft fire so he quickly climbed back into the poor visibility to conceal the FK.8's whereabouts.

However, West was not satisfied that he had accurately pinpointed the enemy's location so he dived down out of the mist again. At this point a flight of seven German scout aircraft appeared and gave chase. One of the Germans scored a direct hit on C8594's cockpit, destroying the wireless and wounding the pilot in the right foot just before he climbed back into the cloud.

Undaunted, West rediscovered the gap and descended once again to overfly the enemy concentration to accurately judge its size and location before he turned for home. Moments later the FK.8 met five more German scouts which dived in to attack from dead ahead. Haslam grabbed his Lewis gun and returned fire but he was no match for the opposition, which raked the RFC machine with bullets. West was hit five more times in the left leg, which smashed the bone and caused blood to gush out.

Levelling out just above the treetops with at least one of the scouts in tow, West twisted his torn trouser leg to produce a makeshift tourniquet. It was obvious that they would never make it back to Vignacourt so once they were safely over the Allied line, West chopped the power and glided to a safe landing near some Canadian troops. They cut the fabric from the side of the aircraft; bound the shaken pilot's almost severed leg and lifted him from the cockpit.

By now West was fading in and out of consciousness but in a moment of lucidity insisted that an 8 Sqn officer be summoned so he could brief them on the location of the enemy troop build-up. No sooner had he relayed the information than he fainted. When he woke up two days later his left leg had been amputated.

On November 8, shortly after his release from Rouen hospital 'Freddy'

**Beauchamp-Proctor flew SE5as similar to this example, which has had its identity obliterated by the War Office's censor**

West was told he was to receive the VC for his actions that day and Haslam would receive the DFC. West was also awarded £250 (around £16,000 in today's money) as compensation for the loss of his leg.

However, the brave pilot was determined to return to flying and in 1919, after purchasing a state-of-the-art replacement leg, he received a permanent commission in the RAF and gradually returned to flying duties.

In 1940 West, by now an Air Commodore, moved to Rome, Italy as the UK's air attaché and later that year he transferred to Switzerland as part of the British Legation in Berne.

From Switzerland he assisted countless Allied airmen who had escaped into the neutral country – so much so that the Nazi Gestapo put a price on his head because of his underground activities. At the end of his second war 'Freddy' West was awarded a CBE by the King prior to 'retiring' and taking up several civilian jobs. He eventually passed away peacefully on July 8, 1988 at the age of 92.

## Canada's Most Decorated

The seventeenth aviator to be awarded the VC was also the third Canadian airman so recognised. 'Billy' Barker finished the war as Canada's most decorated serviceman – with a VC, DSO (& Bar) and the Military Cross (with two Bars) – a record that has never been bettered.

William George 'Billy' Barker was born on the family farm in Dauphin, Manitoba, Canada on November 3, 1894 and enjoyed a horse riding, gun shooting, all-action childhood.

After watching a demonstration by a Wright Brothers' biplane in 1910, Barker developed a lifelong love of aviation, so when war broke out in Europe the young Canadian volunteered for service.

However, his horse and gun skills meant he was initially selected to serve the 1st Canadian Mounted Rifles and he was despatched to Britain with the regiment in June 1915. He then moved to France when the unit deployed on September 22 and it would be December before he finally transferred to the RFC as an observer to with 9 Sqn, which was equipped with BE.2 aircraft at the time.

In early 1916 Barker claimed a Fokker monoplane as shot down in close combat and in April he transferred to 4 Sqn. By July he was with 15 Sqn at Marieux and on July 21 he claimed a Roland two-seater. A second Roland followed on August 15 and on November he spotted a large concentration of some 4,000 German troops massing. He sent an emergency Zone Call, which brought to bear all

Edward Corringham 'Mick' Mannock VC, DSO & Two Bars, MC & Bar (May 24, 1887 – July 26, 1918)

'Mick' Mannock was a confirmed animal lover in addition to being one of the leading aces of the Great War

available artillery fire in the area onto the specified target and changed the course of the Battle of the Somme; action that earned him a Military Cross (MC).

Later that month he applied to become a pilot and was sent to Narborough, Norfolk for training. After just 55 minutes of dual instruction he set off on his first solo flight and by February 1917 he was back in France and ready to restart operational flying at Lealvillers.

Barker had been allocated to 15 Sqn, again flying the decidedly out-dated BE.2, and his first victim was a Fokker scout that he shot down near Cambrai on March 23.

## “ No sooner had he relayed the information than he fainted ”

On April 9, while flying an RE.8 with observer Lt Goodfellow, he helped Australian gunners to range their artillery against a German assault (a job that earned him a 'Bar' to his MC). A second 'Bar' followed in July but in August Barker was injured in the head by shrapnel and sent to Britain to work as a flying instructor.

However, the keen pilot's continual requests for front line service resulted in him being offered a job with a scout unit and the choice of flying SE5as with 56 Sqn or Sopwith Camels with 28 Sqn. He preferred the Camel and following training at Yatesbury, Wiltshire he was posted to Droglandt, near Cambrai, France on October 8.

The same night, while on a 'familiarisation' sortie, Barker led three of his unit across enemy lines and

discovered a flight of enemy aircraft. Moments later he dived headlong into the formation and shot down a German Albatros D.V. He didn't claim the 'kill' as it was an unofficial mission but on October 20 he scored an 'official' kill against an Albatros of Jasta 2. Two more followed on October 27 along with two 'probables.'

In early November the unit transferred (by train) to Italy and 'Billy' Barker was promoted to temporary squadron commander upon his arrival in Milan. He continued to fly and more victories followed in November and December 1917.

The new year started with another victory on January 1 and his string of successes continued to mount – all while flying his personal Camel (B6313), which he had flown since he joined the squadron in England.

A DSO was added to Barker's medal tally in April 1918 but soon afterwards he transferred to 66 Sqn – following his frustration at not being made permanent commander of 28 Sqn.

By July he'd claimed another 16 victories and he then joined the Bristol F.2B-equipped 139 Sqn as its new 'boss' - although he continued to fly his beloved Camel and soon won a 'Bar' to his DSO. By September Camel B6313 had become the most successful fighter aircraft in the history of the RAF having shot down 46 aircraft and balloons and accumulated 404 hours since September 1917.

On September 30, after flying 900 combat hours in two and a half years, Barker was transferred back to Britain to command the fighter training school at Hounslow Heath. But yet again he convinced his superiors that he needed to return to the battlefront. The persuasive pilot was granted a short, ten-day, 'refresher tour' with 201 Sqn in France where he was allocated an example of the new Sopwith Snipe (E8102).

The Snipe was not a fast aircraft by the standards of its time, but its excellent climb and manoeuvrability made it a good match for contemporary German fighters. That said, by the end of his tour Barker had not managed to add any more victories to his tally and on October 27, 1918 he flew E8102 back to the aircraft depot at Hounslow at 21,000ft (6,400m).

However, the determined Barker was not about to give up and at 8.25am he spotted a two-seat Rumpler in the area of Forêt de Mormal and he swiftly downed it with the Snipe's two Vickers guns. But for once 'Billy' Barker was careless and he failed to see a Fokker D.VII, which attacked him from below. The Snipe was damaged and Barker was wounded in the right thigh but he soon downed the German by way of revenge.

In the meantime a large group of at least 15 other D.VIIs from Jasta 24 and Jasta 44 had appeared and quickly engaged in a fight with the Snipe. In the twisting, descending battle Barker was wounded three times in the legs, then his left elbow was blown away. Yet he was still able to single-handedly shoot or drive down three enemy aircraft before making a forced landing just inside Allied lines.

He was taken to hospital in Rouen and a few days later was informed that he had now added a VC to his impressive haul of medals. In mid-January 1919 he was transported back to England and on March 1 he hobbled into Buckingham Palace to receive his medal from the King.

'Billy' Barker returned to Canada in May 1919 as the most decorated Canadian of the war, with the Victoria Cross, the Distinguished Service Order and Bar; the Military Cross and two Bars; two Italian Silver Medals for Military Valour, and the French Croix de Guerre. He was also mentioned in despatches three times. He was officially credited with one balloon captured, two (and seven shared) balloons destroyed, 33 (and two shared) aircraft destroyed, and five aircraft 'out of control.' He had the highest 'destroyed' ratio for any RAF, RFC or RNAS pilot during the conflict.

After the war Barker formed Bishop-Barker Aeroplanes with fellow Victoria Cross recipient and Canadian ace Billy Bishop. He then joined the Royal Canadian Air Force (RCAF) but died on March 12, 1930 when he lost control of his Fairchild KR-21 biplane during an airshow at Rockcliffe, near Ottawa, Ontario.

**'Mick' Mannock was promoted to Major and chosen to succeed 'Billy' Bishop in command of 85 Sqn. These 85 Sqn SE5a aircraft are lined up at St Omer in June 1918**

Officers of the RAF's 1 Sqn with their SE5a aircraft at Clairmarais near St Omer, France on July 3, 1918

## South Africa's Leading Ace

The honour of being the eighteenth aviator to receive the VC fell to South Africa's leading Ace of the war.

Andrew Frederick Weatherby Beauchamp-Proctor was born in the South African Cape on September 4, 1894. When war erupted in 1914, Beauchamp-Proctor took leave from his engineering studies at the University of Cape Town to join the Duke of Edinburgh's Own Rifles.

He served as a signalman in the German South-West Africa campaign and in August 1915 he was demobilised with an honourable discharge. He managed to complete his third year of studies before re-enlisting, this time with the RFC in March 1917.

Beauchamp-Proctor arrived in England on March 26 and following ground school began his pilot training at Castle Bromwich, near Birmingham in May. He succeeded in learning to fly despite his diminutive stature of 5ft 2in (1.57m), which meant his seat had to be raised so he could see out of the cockpit. Wooden blocks were also fastened to his rudder bar so he could reach the pedals.

## "Camel B6313 became the most successful fighter aircraft in the history of the RAF"

Upon achieving his 'wings' in July 1917 the new pilot and was posted to 84 Sqn at Beaulieu, Hampshire where he began to train on the SE5a scout.

The unit moved to Flez, France in September but Beauchamp-Proctor's first action did not occur until November 22 when he and a colleague shared the destruction of an observation kite while flying SE5a B597. A week later he forced a German two-seater out of the skies and despatched another in a vertical dive on December 5. From this point forward victories came at a steady rate and in March 1918 alone he scored eight 'kills.'

In June Beauchamp-Proctor was awarded the Military Cross for his on-going service, particularly an attack on three German scouts on May 19 that saw him downing one and causing the

other two to collide in mid-air.

July would pass without incident and on August 3 Beauchamp-Proctor was granted one of the first ever DFCs for "destroying 13 enemy machines and bringing down 13 more out of control in a period of a few months." By the end of the month he had scored an additional 14 aircraft, increasing his tally of claims to 43 – most scored in his personal modified SE5a D6856.

Beauchamp-Proctor's final operational sortie came on October 8, 1918 when he downed a Rumpler near Maretz. Moments later he was engaged by eight German aircraft and in the ensuing combat he was wounded badly in the arm. By the time he was fit to return to flying the war was over.

By the end of the conflict his total tally was 54 victories; consisting of 22 enemy aircraft and 16 balloons destroyed as well as 16 enemy aircraft downed completely out of control. His 16 balloons downed made him the leading British Empire 'balloon buster'

On November 2 Beauchamp-Proctor was awarded the DSO for his flying against balloons and on November 30 he was told he would be receiving the Victoria Cross or his entire war effort.

Post war the South African embarked on a four-month-long lecture tour of the USA in March 1919, before returning to England and re-joining the RAF as a Flight Lieutenant.

On June 21, 1921 Andrew Beauchamp-Proctor was killed when his Sopwith Snipe (E8220) crashed while performing a loop while practising for the RAF Air Pageant at Hendon.

## The RFC's Final VC

The nineteenth and final VC awarded to a member of the Royal Flying Corps was presented to Edward 'Mick' Mannock. Although the award related to flying during the latter days of the Great War it was only after intensive lobbying that the popular pilot was posthumously granted the medal on July 18, 1919.

Edward Corringham 'Mick' Mannock was born in Britain to Irish parents on May 24, 1887 but proved to be a sickly child and was almost blind in one eye. He also received little in the way of education and at the age of 13 he was sent out to work to provide income for his family, which was almost destitute after his father left his mother to bring up four children singlehandedly.

When war broke out in 1914 Mannock was working as a telephone engineer in Turkey and after the Ottoman Empire's entry into the war he found himself interned. Conditions in the internment camp was very poor and Mannock and his co-inhabitants were soon sick with fever and malnutrition. It was only the interjection by the American Consulate that secured the 'prisoners' release and Mannock returned to Britain where he was deemed 'unfit for military service.'

However, 'Mick' recovered sufficiently to join the Royal Army Medical Corps and then the Royal Engineers but in August 1916 he applied to join the RFC as a pilot.

Initial pilot training took place at Hendon followed by advanced instruction at Upavon and he qualified on November 28.

Throughout this period Mannock had managed to conceal his defective sight and after operational training he was assigned to 40 Sqn at Aire, Lens, France in April 1917.

Initially, 'Mick' failed to make many friends on the squadron; his lower class roots not endearing him to the predominantly ex-public school pilots. He later recalled that he preferred being in the air fighting the enemy than being in the crew room with his colleagues. However, when a lower wing detached from his Nieuport 23 Scout on April 19, his skilful flying not only enabled him to land safely, it also finally won him respect from his peers.

Then, on May 7, he scored his first aerial victory – a kite balloon. His second success came exactly a month later when he shot down an Albatros D.III and two days later he scored two more victories.

## " His total tally was 54 victories "

On July 19 Mannock was awarded the Military Cross and in October he received a 'Bar' to add to the medal.

By the end of 1917 'Mick' Mannock's tally stood at 16 enemy aircraft downed and he had been sent back to Britain to join 74 Sqn, which was equipping with the new SE5a at London Colney. Mannock was appointed commander of A Flight and on March 1 the unit flew across the Channel to its new base at Teteghem near Dunkirk. A month later it moved again, this time to La Lovie airfield near Poperinghe.

On April 12 Mannock scored the unit's first victory when he claimed an Albatros downed near Carvin. The following month he claimed no fewer than 24 victories and on May 19 he received the DSO. Amazingly a 'Bar' had been added to the DSO by the end of the same month and he started the following month with three kills on June 1 alone!

On June 21 'Mick' was promoted to Major and chosen to succeed 'Billy' Bishop in command of 85 Sqn; a job he started on July 3.

He scored his first victory with the squadron on July 7 when he destroyed a Fokker D.VII, sent another down out of control and forced two more to collide in mid-air. He had another victory on July 8; one on July 10; two on July 14; another one on July 19; two more on July 20 and, finally, a Fokker Dr.I on July 22.

Four days later Mannock took off from St Omer in SE5a E1295 at just after 5.00am. He was joined in the air by a young New Zealander called Donald Inglis, who was flying SE5a E1294. Inglis had yet to achieve his first victory and 'Mick' invited him to tag along on a mission to offer him some tips.

Both aircraft remained below 50ft (15m) en route to the battlefront until Inglis noticed Mannock suddenly climb near Lestrem. 'Mick' had seen a German DFW C.V biplane and immediately began the attack. The reconnaissance aircraft soon fell to the combined gunnery of the two SE5as and Mannock would later be credited with a share of the kill – it would be his 61st and final victory.

Then, contrary to his usual advice, Mannock descended down to low-level over the trenches. It is thought he was trying to view the wreckage of the crashed DFW but soon his aircraft came under a barrage of fire from German anti-aircraft guns. Trailing close behind, Inglis noted flames appear from Mannock's engine cowling and as the flames began to spread the SE5a crashed into German occupied territory. The aircraft exploded and the legend that was Major 'Mick' Mannock is thought to have died instantly. The body of the 31-year-old pilot was never recovered.

Mannock was among the most decorated men in the British Armed Forces. He was honoured with the Military Cross twice, was one of the rare three-time recipients of the Distinguished Service Order, but after the Armistice, in November 1918, many felt it was unjust that Mannock had not been awarded the VC. An official investigation by the RAF proved the gallant pilot had actually 'under-claimed' his kills and could legitimately have stated a total of 73 combat victories. The same report stated that he should have been awarded the highest available recognition and in the summer of 1919 the newly appointed Air Minister – Mr Winston Churchill MP – recommended that the King should, indeed, award Mannock a posthumous VC.

Finally, on July 18, 1919, Mannock's remarkable story appeared alongside his citation in the London Gazette. It would be the last VC awarded to a pilot for valour shown during the 1914–1918 War. ❖

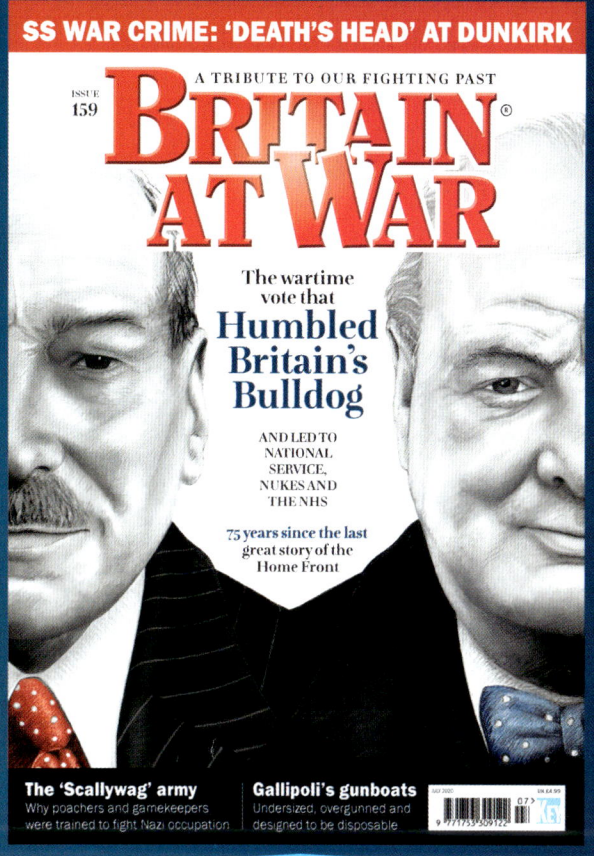

# Joint Recipients of the RAF's First VCs of World War Two

## The first two Victoria Crosses of World War Two were awarded to the bridge busting crew of a 12 Sqn Fairey Battle. Yet their gunner went unrewarded

The RAF's 12 Sqn moved into France during the opening days of World War Two and by May 1940 its single-engined Fairey Battle bombers were involved in combat with German forces that were advancing through the Low Countries in a Blitzkrieg movement.

On May 12 the squadron was tasked with destroying vital bridges over the Albert Canal in Belgium. The entire squadron volunteered for the mission but it was decided that the six crews already detailed on the readiness roster should undertake the potentially hazardous mission.

The first section of three aircraft was to be led by Flying Officer Donald Garland piloting Battle P2204 - coded PH-K. Joining him in the aircraft was Observer/Navigator Sgt Tom Gray and Leading Aircraftman (LAC) Lawrence Reynolds, the latter serving as rear gunner during their low-level attack on the Veldwezelt Bridge.

## Garland

Donald Edward Garland was born in Ballincor, County Wicklow, Ireland on June 28, 1918. He was the youngest of four sons fathered by Dr Patrick Garland who had served with distinction as a surgeon during the Boer War. Sadly all four boys would be killed or seriously injured in RAF service during World War Two.

Donald graduated from Cardinal Vaughan Memorial School at Holland Park in London in 1935 with a good all-round School Certificate and after working in an insurance office, he joined the RAF on a short-term commission in July 1937.

He was soon accepted for elementary flying training at RAF Hamble, Hampshire and awarded the rank of Pilot Officer upon his graduation in May 1938.

His first posting was to 12 Sqn, which was then based at RAF Andover, Hampshire in the day bomber role and in the process of converting from the Hawker Hind biplane to the Fairey Battle monoplane.

Garland was promoted to Flying Officer status in August 1939 just prior to being posted to France, where 12 Sqn operated from a small cornfield near Barry-au-Bac.

**Donald Edward Garland VC (June 28, 1918 – May 12, 1940)**

**Thomas Gray VC (May 17, 1914 – May 12, 1940)**

## Gray

Thomas Gray was born in Urchfont, Wiltshire on May 17, 1914, the fourth of seven sons of the village policeman. Five of the boys enlisted in the RAF with Tom joining as a Halton 'Brat' on August 27, 1929 to train as an engine fitter.

He left Halton, Buckinghamshire in 1932 and was posted to 40 Sqn where he soon volunteered to fly as an air gunner on Fairey Gordon bombers. A year later he was promoted to Leading Aircraftsman and posted to 15 Sqn with Hawker Hinds.

On March 1937 he joined 58 Sqn at RAF Driffield, Yorkshire with the large Vickers Virginia bomber and in February 1938 he transferred to 12 Sqn at RAF Andover and was promoted to Corporal following training as an observer at No 1 Air Observers School. A further promotion followed in January 1939 when he became a Sergeant.

## Bridge Busters

On that fateful day on May 12, 1940 Garland and Gray (along with gunner Reynolds) were tasked to bomb the Veldwezelt Bridge, which the German infantry had captured some days earlier.

Just prior to 9.00am the five Battles were prepared for take-off

from the grass airfield near the village of Amifontaine, France, where the squadron had been based since December 1939. Garland was to lead a flight of three aircraft into the skies and was joined by wingmen Pilot Officer I A McIntosh (flying Battle L5439) and Sgt Fred Marland (in L5227) as they set off towards the target.

Meanwhile, Pilot Officers Norman Thomas (flying Battle P2332) and T.D.H. Davy (in L5241) were tasked with attacking an equally important bridge in nearby Vroenhoven.

Ahead of the Battles was a flight of eight Hawker Hurricanes from 1 Sqn that was intended to provide top cover for the attack on the bridges. However, the presence of a large number of Messerschmitt Bf109 fighters from the crack Jagdgeschwader 27 (JG 27) caught the Allies by surprise and the Hurricanes were soon swamped and unable to provide any protection to the lightly armed Battle bombers.

Thomas and Davy were the first to reach their target but both had endured a terrifying gauntlet of anti-aircraft flak and Luftwaffe fighters. Thomas was shot down and captured while Davy ordered his crew to bail out of their stricken Battle before he nursed the bomber back behind French lines.

The Fairey Battle was developed as a monoplane successor to the earlier Hawker Hart and Hind biplanes. It was powered by the same Rolls-Royce Merlin engine used in the various fighters but the Battle was weighed down with a three-man crew and a bomb load. It was therefore slow, limited in range and highly vulnerable to both anti-aircraft fire and hostile fighters

## The High Price of Victory

Shortly afterwards Garland, leading the second section, reached the Veldwezelt area just below the 1,000ft (305m) cloud base and began a shallow bombing run on the bridge through an almost impenetrable wall of flak. It was later estimated that around 300 anti-aircraft guns had been entrenched around the bridge in a defensive ring. Undeterred, Garland and his crew pressed on with their attack until they hit the bridge; much of the success being attributed to the coolness of the pilot.

Sadly, shortly after the bridge had been bombed P2204 was hit and it crashed, killing all three aboard. McIntosh's Battle was also hit and the main fuel tank caught ablaze. He jettisoned his bombs and made a forced landing but the crew became prisoners of war. Marland's Battle successfully released its bombs but then climbed, seemingly out of control before rolling over and diving into the ground.

After the raid, local civilians recovered the badly burnt bodies of Garland, Gray and Reynolds and quickly buried them in a secret location to prevent the Germans claiming them. Near the end of the war Allied authorities were notified and all three airmen were re-interred in Lanaken cemetery in Belgium. They were subsequently moved to the Imperial War Graves Commission cemetery at Haverlee, near Leuven, Belgium.

Despite the high cost of life the mission had been a success and the western end of the bridge was destroyed. Evidence suggested the damage had been specifically caused by Garland and Gray's attack. It had been Gray's first operational bombing raid and they were both posthumously awarded the Victoria Cross.

In the 1960s the RAF named Vickers VC10 XR807, serving with 101 Sqn, *Donald Garland VC & Thomas Gray VC* in memory of the two airmen and in 2005 an RAF Tornado GR.4 from 12 Sqn carried the duo's name beneath the cockpit as part of the squadron's 90th anniversary celebrations.

After the war there was consternation when it was discovered that the third member of the crew, 20-year old gunner LAC Lawrence Reynolds who was also killed and buried alongside his crewmates, received no commendation whatsoever. It was later described as 'one of the great injustices of the war'.

By May 1940, the Battle had suffered heavy losses and frequently in excess of 50% aircraft failed to return per mission. By the end of 1940, the type had been entirely withdrawn from active combat service

More than 2,000 Battles were built but the type was far from popular with its crews

Garland and Grey's Battle was registered P2204 and wore the PH-K codes of 12 Sqn

*Andy Hay/www.flyingart.co.uk*

## CITATION

**Flying Officer Donald Edward Garland (40105) – 12 Sqn RAF**     **Sergeant Thomas Gray (563627) – 12 Sqn RAF**

'The King has been graciously pleased to confer the Victoria Cross on the mentioned officer and non-commissioned officer in recognition of most conspicuous bravery.

F/O Garland was the pilot and Sgt Gray was the observer of the leading aircraft of a formation of five aircraft that attacked a bridge over the Albert Canal which had not been destroyed and was allowing the enemy to advance into Belgium. All the aircrews of the squadron concerned volunteered for the operation, and, after five crews had been selected by drawing lots, the attack was delivered at low altitude against this vital target. Orders were issued that this bridge was to be destroyed at all costs. As had been expected, exceptionally intense machine-gun and anti-aircraft fire were encountered. Moreover, the bridge area was heavily protected by enemy fighters. In spite of this, the formation successfully delivered a dive-bombing attack from the lowest practicable altitude. British fighters in the vicinity reported that the target was obscured by the bombs bursting on it and near it. Only one of the five aircraft concerned returned from this mission. The pilot of this aircraft reports that besides being subjected to extremely heavy anti-aircraft fire, through which they dived to attack the objective, our aircraft were also attacked by a large number of enemy fighters after they had released their bombs on the target. Much of the success of this vital operation must be attributed to the formation leader, F/O Garland, and to the coolness and resource of Sgt Gray, who in most difficult conditions navigated F/O Garland's aircraft in such a manner that the whole formation was able successfully to attack the target in spite of subsequent heavy losses. F/O Garland and Sgt Gray did not return.'

[*London Gazette* – June 11, 1940]

# Bomber Command's First VC

## Of the 32 VCs awarded during World War Two, 19 went to members of RAF Bomber Command. The first was given to Flt Lt (later Wg Cmdr) Roderick Learoyd

Along with many of his comrades, Roderick Alastair Brook Learoyd was not an obvious candidate for the supreme honour of a Victoria Cross.

He was born in Folkestone, Kent on February 5, 1913; the son of an Army Major, and was educated at Hydreye House Prep School in Sussex and later Wellington College in Berkshire before attending Chelsea College of Aeronautical and Automobile Engineering.

There followed a short spell in Argentina as a fruit farmer and a period as a motor engineer before Learoyd decided to join the RAF and learn to fly. He was accepted for pilot training in March 1936 on a short service commission and undertook his ab initio flying at Hamble, Hampshire.

Learoyd's first posting was to 49 Sqn, flying Hawker Hind biplane day-bombers out of RAF Worthy Down, Hampshire but in March 1938 the unit moved to RAF Scampton, Lincolnshire to begin converting onto the new Handley Page Hampden. The all-metal twin-engined monoplanes provided a quantum shift in capabilities and by early 1939 the unit was fully operational with the new bombers.

**Roderick Alastair Brook Learoyd VC (February 5, 1913 –January 24, 1996)**

## Two-Hour Readiness

Later in the year the squadron was brought to 'two-hour readiness' as the political climate across Europe darkened and on September 3 the unit flew its first operational sortie providing armed reconnaissance over the North Sea looking for German naval vessels. Just three aircraft were involved in the mission, one of which was flown by Acting Flt Lt Roderick Learoyd.

Over the course of the next ten months Learoyd undertook a further 23 bombing missions, including several attacks on the heavily defended Dortmund Ems canal. He was assigned this target again on August 12, 1940 when eleven Hampdens from 49 Sqn were tasked with destroying an aqueduct carrying the canal north of Munster.

The canal was known to be of special importance in view of the essential build-up of barges and other shipping in the area - particularly for the German's planned Channel ports invasion.

In view of this the Germans had provided overwhelming defences in the form of hundreds of anti-aircraft guns and masses of searchlights.

Of the aircraft and crews selected for the mission, four were to bomb diversionary targets while the remainder were tasked to bomb the canal at specific times to activate the ten-minute delayed action fuses on their special canister bombs.

Learoyd's first posting was to RAF Worthy Down, Hampshire to fly Hawker Hind biplane day-bombers similar to these

The all-metal twin-engined Hampden monoplanes provided a quantum shift in capabilities over the earlier biplanes and 49 Sqn was fully operational with the new bombers by early 1939

Learoyd's Hampden was registered P4403 and carried the 49 Sqn codes EA-M. The aircraft was named *Pinocchio* and carried a depiction of the Walt Disney character below the left side of the cockpit

Andy Hay/www.flyingart.co.uk

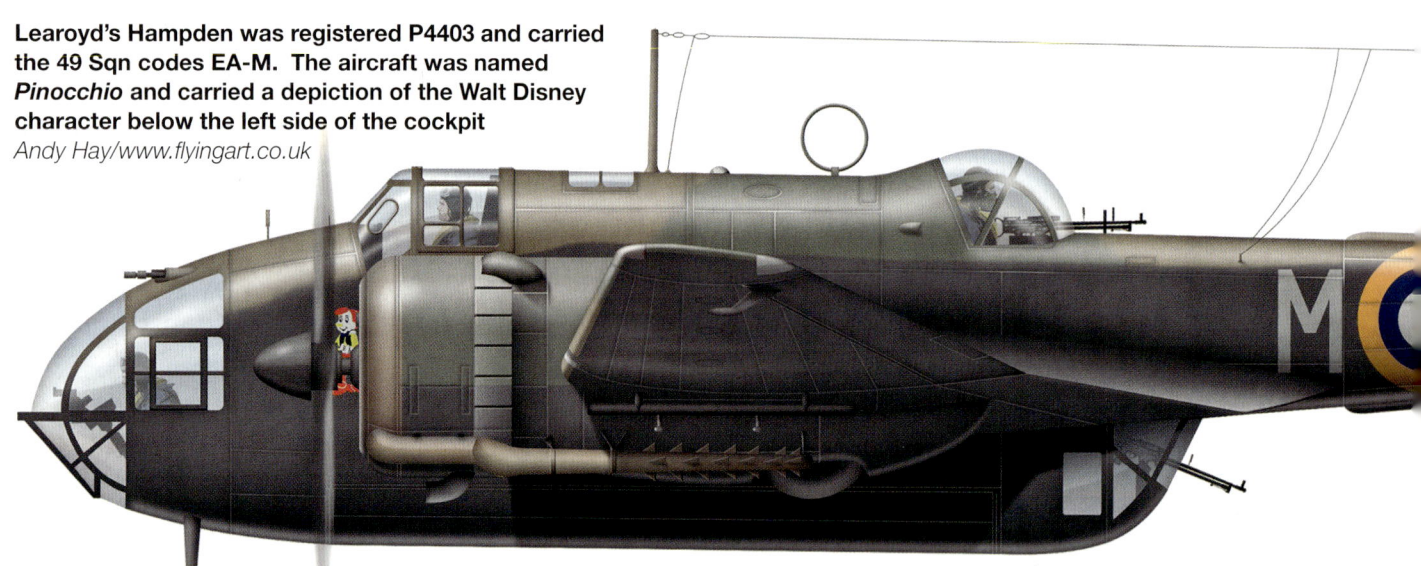

For this sortie Learoyd had been allocated Hampden P4403 EA-M. The aircraft was named *Pinocchio* and carried a depiction of the Walt Disney character below the left side of the cockpit. His crew comprised of P/O John Lewis (Navigator and Bomb Aimer), Sgt J Ellis (Wireless Operator and Dorsal Air Gunner) and LAC Rich – the latter serving as Ventral Air Gunner.

Learoyd's aircraft was due over the target at exactly 11.23pm and would be the last of five to attack the aqueduct. He eased the heavily loaded bomber off Scampton's grass runway at precisely 8.00pm and climbed into the clear night, steering towards Germany. Lewis' navigation skills got the crew

to their holding point with ten minutes to spare and they circled in the half moonlight, waiting for the exact time to attack the target.

## Diversionary Tactics

Meanwhile, out of sight to Learoyd, four other Hampdens were making their diversion raids and a further two were bombing Texel Island, having failed to find their planned targets.

Then it was time to begin the attack on the canal and Learoyd looked on as Sqn Ldr 'Jamie' Pitcairn-Hill DFC began the first bombing run in Hampden P4402. He was met with intense anti-aircraft flak and bright searchlights as he flew down the canal at 100ft

maintaining a rock-steady course for his bomb aimer. Despite taking multiple hits, the aircraft managed to escape the area and limp home to Scampton.

The second and third aircraft were not so lucky. Hampden P4410, flown by Australian P/O E H Ross crashed into the canal amidst a barrage of flak and P4340 (flown by fellow Australian pilot F/O A R Mulligan) was also hit. The latter climbed away and the crew bailed out but were later captured by the Germans and taken prisoner.

The fourth Hampden (flown by P/O Matthews) successfully dropped its bombs but staggered home on one engine – and then it was Learoyd's turn to attack.

## Hit by Flak

Just six minutes after Pitcairn-Hill had alerted the Germans to the unit's intentions, Learoyd began a shallow dive towards the canal at 150ft (46m). By now the anti-aircraft gunners had perfected their range and the Hampden received the full brunt of the weapons. Learoyd ducked below the cockpit frame and flew solely on instruments according to the directions of his bomb aimer Lewis. Meanwhile, both gunners began to spray ammunition towards the searchlights as they passed by.

As they approached the aqueduct, a direct hit from a shell left a large hole in the starboard wing and almost immediately a second shell passed through the same wing between the Bristol Pegasus engine and the cockpit.

Machine gun fire continued to strike the aircraft but eventually Lewis was in the correct position to release his bomb load and Learoyd hauled the aircraft up and away from the guns.

As they cleared the area the crew took stock of the situation. They had suffered a serious hit to the hydraulic system, which caused the flaps to deploy, but the shell damage to the wing had fortunately missed the fuel tanks.

## " Learoyd ducked below the cockpit frame and flew solely on instruments "

## Safely Home

Shortly after 2.00am on August 13, the Hampden crossed the English coast and was soon overhead its base at RAF Scampton. Learoyd decided that the damage was too severe to contemplate a night landing so he circled the airfield for a further three hours until first light and belly-landed safely just before 5.00am.

Post-attack reconnaissance showed that the raid had been a complete success and the canal was out of action for ten days.

For his high courage, skill and determination, Learoyd was awarded the Victoria Cross.

Roderick Learoyd survived the war and became a Wing Commander prior to being demobilised in 1946. A career flying with the Malayan Civil Aviation Department followed, along with a lengthy period working for the Austin Motor Company. He passed away peacefully on January 24, 1996 at the age of 82; his obituary noting that, 'He was a quiet and reserved man but also a friendly and comradely one. A good man at a party, but never allowing social life to interrupt his fighting career. Even after the award of the VC he gave no hint of conceit or self- importance.' ❖

**The Hampden carried a crew of four and was powered by a pair of Bristol Pegasus radial engines**

# Fighter Command's Lone VC

## Although 32 Victoria Crosses were awarded to RAF airmen during World War Two, just one was given to a Fighter Command pilot. That man was James Nicolson

During the Great War of 1914-1918 it appeared that airmen were awarded the VC for their high tallies of aerial victories. Conversely, during World War Two the only RAF fighter pilot to receive the VC didn't have a 'kill' to his name.

Eric James Brindley Nicolson (more commonly known by either his middle name of James or his nickname 'Nick') was born in Hampstead, London in 1917 and was educated at Tonbridge School in Kent.

He started a career in engineering in Shoreham, West Sussex in 1935 but a year later he opted to enlist in the RAF. Flying training began at the civilian school at White Waltham, Berkshire that October before Nicolson completed his service training at RAF Ternhill, Shropshire and joined his first squadron, 72 Sqn, at RAF Church Fenton, Yorkshire flying the Gloster Gladiator.

### A 'Natural' Pilot

Nicolson was described as a 'natural' pilot with 'above average' ability and an extrovert and gregarious nature.

In April 1939 the squadron began to receive its first Supermarine Spitfires and by October the type had replaced the Gladiator in 72 Sqn service. Nicolson – by now a Flt Lt – soon converted onto the new type and flew his first operational missions when the unit moved to RAF Leconfield later that month, although he saw no combat.

The squadron continued to live a nomadic lifestyle and Nicolson moved with it to Drem (Scotland), Church Fenton and Acklington (Northumberland) but had still seen no combat by the time he was posted to the newly formed 249 Sqn on May 15, 1940 as Acting Flight Commander. A month later the squadron traded its Spitfires in for Hawker Hurricanes and was declared operational at the end of July prior to moving south to RAF Boscombe Down, Hampshire to play its part in the Battle of Britain.

### Operational

By the middle of August Flt Lt Nicolson had still seen little in the way of combat but that was all to change on August 16.

Flying Hurricane P3576 GN-A as the leader of a three-ship formation using

**Eric James Brindley Nicolson VC DFC (April 29, 1917 – May 2, 1945)**

the call-sign 'Red Section' he took off from Boscombe Down with orders to patrol the Poole, Ringwood and Salisbury area. He was joined by P/O M A King (flying P3616 GN-F) and Sqn Ldr E B King – the latter a supernumerary officer attached to the squadron to obtain combat experience. None of them had yet fired a shot in anger.

Nicolson climbed to 15,000ft (4,572m) in a gin clear summer sky and soon spotted three Junkers Ju-88s. He led Red Section towards their target but as he closed within a mile he had to reluctantly abandon the chase when a large formation of Spitfires began to tackle the Luftwaffe bombers.

Undeterred, Nicolson climbed to 18,000ft (5,486m) to re-join the rest of the 249 Sqn aircraft but as he was locating the other Hurricanes he and his wingmen felt their aircraft jolt as they took direct hits from a burst of German cannon shells fired by a marauding flight of Messerschmitt Bf109 *Emils*.

Sqn Ldr King's aircraft entered a spin but the pilot was able to recover and land back safely, shaken but unhurt. P/O King was not so lucky. His Hurricane burst into flames and although he bailed out safely, a Royal Artillery battalion took aim at what they assumed to be an enemy pilot and shot his parachute canopy to pieces. King plunged to his death.

### Shot Up and Going Down

Meanwhile, Nicolson found himself in great danger. His Hurricane had been hit by four shells – one of which had shattered the canopy Perspex

**Eric James Brindley Nicolson VC (centre) taken at the hospital where he was recuperating from wounds sustained in the action in which he won his VC**

Nicholson's Hurricane comes under fire at 18,000ft over Southern England on August 16, 1940
Andy Hay/www.flyingart.co.uk

In the 1980s the Battle of Britain Memorial flight painted Hurricane LF363 in Nicolson's markings and in 2015, to mark the 75th anniversary of the Battle of Britain the RAF painted a Eurofighter Typhoon in similar colours. The Typhoon is seen here flying with Battle of Britain veteran Spitfire P7350 at the 2015 Royal International Air Tattoo *Steve Bridgewater*

and a shard had punctured his left eyelid. A second shell hit the fuel tank in the fuselage; a third went straight through the fuselage's fabric covering and ripped Nicolson's trouser leg to shreds. The final shell hit him in the right foot.

Although in great pain he was able to put the aircraft into a right hand spiral to try to escape the Bf109s and as the fuel tank caught fire, he began the bail out procedure.

With flames now licking from behind the cockpit instrument panel, Nicolson was about to leave the aircraft when he suddenly saw a Messerschmitt Bf110 twin-engined fighter in front of his windscreen. The gun sight was still working and Nicolson 'saw red.' He dropped back into his seat and pressed the trigger, letting loose a stream of tracer that raked into the German aircraft.

The Luftwaffe pilot tried to evade the Hurricane but by now Nicolson was intent on shooting it down and was oblivious to the pain. He looked down at the throttle lever in his left hand and noticed his flesh melting but still he pressed on with the attack. Only when the heat began to burn his face did he break off the dogfight.

## Bailing Out

Now Nicolson needed to evacuate the aircraft as quickly as possible and he pushed himself up and out of the seat once again – only to bang his head on the still closed canopy. He reached up and slid the canopy open then tried again to leave the cockpit. Nicolson eventually re      alised he was still strapped into his seat so he slumped back down again and tried to undo his harness. One strap unbuckled easily but another was burnt and needed to be snapped before he could finally drop from the aircraft, which was now inverted at 12,000ft (3,658m).

Diving headfirst towards the ground, he pulled the ripcord to deploy his parachute, which fortunately opened without drama.

At that second a German fighter sped past the parachute and promptly turned back towards him. Fearing the Luftwaffe pilot might fire at him Nicolson elected to let himself hang limply under the canopy pretending to be dead. It worked and the Messerschmitt flew off to look for trouble elsewhere.

## Burned and Battered

As he floated slowly to earth Nicolson was finally able to take stock of his injuries, which included severe burns to both hands and his face as well as a bullet wound to his left foot and damage to his left eye.

However, he was still alert enough to steer his parachute inland to avoid landing in the English Channel (and almost certainly drowning in his condition) and also swerved a high-tension cable. Unfortunately, as Nicolson was preparing to land, he too became the victim of friendly fire when a member of the Home Guard shot him in the buttock with a 12-bore!

Nicolson lay in a farmer's field, unable to use his hands to release himself from his harness, until he was rescued and taken to Southampton Hospital. Three weeks later he was moved to the RAF Hospital at Halton, Buckinghamshire for specialised burns treatment.

For his exceptional gallantry and disregard for the safety of his own life, James Nicolson was awarded the Victoria Cross on November 15, 1940. He was notified of the award by telegram and reportedly told a fellow patient, "Now I'll have to earn it…" Ten days later he was deemed well enough to travel to Buckingham Palace to receive his cross from the King.

## Back to Flying

Although he was not medically fit to return to full flying duties, Nicolson joined 54 OTU as an instructor in February 1941 and in November was assigned to 1459 Flight at Hibaldstow, Lincolnshire flying the experimental Douglas Havoc 'Turbinlite' night fighter.

Six months later he was posted to India to fly the Bristol Beaufighter and de Havilland Mosquito and received the Distinguished Flying Cross (DFC) for his various ground attack sorties against the Japanese in the region.

By April 1945 Nicolson had become a Wing Commander and was awarded a desk job with RAF Burma Headquarters but he still itched for flying opportunities. On May 2 he convinced the crew of a 355 Sqn Consolidated B-24 Liberator (KH210) to take him along on a mission as an 'observer.' The aircraft crashed in the Indian Ocean and no sign of Nicolson was ever found. He was just 28 years old. ❖

Nicolson's Hurricane was registered P3576 and wore 249 Sqn markings as GN-A *Andy Hay/www.flyingart.co.uk*

In April 1983 James Nicolson's son (also called James) sold his father's VC to support his elderly mother and to protest about meagre war widow pensions. Today his VC can be seen at the RAF Museum in Hendon while the badly burned uniform and 'Mae West' he wore as his Hawker Hurricane burned can be seen at Tangmere Museum, near Chichester *Via Andy Saunders*

## CITATION

### Flight Lieutenant Eric James Brindley Nicolson (39329) – 249 Sqn RAF

'The King has been graciously pleased to confer the Victoria Cross on the following officer in recognition of most conspicuous bravery.

'During an engagement with the enemy near Southampton on August 16, 1940, Flt Lt Nicolson's aircraft was hit by four cannon shells, two of which wounded him whilst another set fire to the gravity tank. When about to abandon his aircraft owing to flames in the cockpit he sighted an enemy fighter. This he attacked and shot down, although as a result of staying in his burning aircraft he sustained serious burns to his hands, face, neck and legs. Flt Lt Nicolson has always displayed great enthusiasm for air fighting and this incident shows that he possesses courage and determination of a high order. By continuing to engage the enemy after he had been wounded and his aircraft set on fire, he displayed exceptional gallantry and disregard for the safety of his own life.'

[*London Gazette* – November 15, 1940]

# The Youngest Hero

## When John Hannah was awarded the Victoria Cross in 1940 he was just 18 years of age – making him the youngest member of aircrew to ever receive the medal

John Hannah was born in Paisley, Scotland on November 27, 1921 and following education in Glasgow he joined the RAF in 1939 at the outbreak of war and trained as a wireless operator.

At the completion of his studies he was promoted to Sergeant and assigned to 83 Sqn in 1940 as a wireless operator/gunner on Handley Page Hampden bombers.

On September 15, 1940 – while the Battle of Britain was raging over much of southern England – Hannah was part of P/O C A Conner's crew aboard Hampden P1355 – coded OL-W – as it flew across the Channel to launch a successful attack on German shipping near Antwerp, Belgium.

As part of a flight of 15 aircraft from 83 Sqn, P1355 took off from RAF Scampton, Lincolnshire at 10.30pm and set course for the barges, which were reported to be part of an armada of sea-going vessels for the threatened invasion of Britain.

The bombers were caught in searchlights as they approached their target and, shortly after the crew of P1355 had released its bombs, the Hampden was hit with shrapnel, bullets and an incendiary shell that exploded in the vicinity of the bomb bay.

The aircraft caught fire and with the flames spreading rapidly, the rear gunner and navigator were forced to bale out over occupied Europe – the latter through the cockpit floor that had melted beneath his feet.

Sgt Hannah had the option to bale out but he bravely chose to stay aboard the aircraft to fight the fire. He first used the bomber's two extinguishers and when they were exhausted he resorted to using his logbook and bare hands

**John Hannah VC (November 27, 1921 – June 7, 1947)**

to beat out the flames. The sheer heat from the flames also began to detonate the Hampden's ammunition within their cases so Hannah quickly disposed of them by throwing them out through the hole in the fuselage.

Despite sustaining terrible injuries to his face and hands he was successful in extinguishing the blaze and P/O Conner and navigator Sgt Hayhurst were able to bring the almost wrecked aircraft back safely. Upon landing Hannah was immediately transferred to hospital for emergency treatment and he was still a patient when he was informed of his award.

Sgt John Hannah attended Buckingham Palace on October 10, 1940 for an investiture ceremony where he was presented with his award. He was just 18 years old and the youngest aviator ever to receive the VC.

P/O Conner received the Distinguished Flying Cross and Sgt Hayhurst, navigator and bomb-aimer, received the Distinguished Flying Medal for the part they played in the raid.

Undoubtedly brought on by his weakened condition due to his severe burns, Hannah contracted tuberculosis and was forced to give up work in 1943. He died on June 7, 1947 and was buried at St James the Great Church in Birstall, where his headstone is inscribed: 'Courageous Duty Done In Love, He Serves His Pilot Now Above. ❖

The Handley Page HP.52 Hampden twin-engined medium bomber first flew in 1936 and bore the brunt of the early bombing war over Europe. However, as the war went on, it became clear that the Hampden was unsuited to modern combat missions and, after a period of mainly operating at night, it was retired from Bomber Command service in late 1942

John Hannah's Hampden I was registered P1355 and wore the OL-W codes of 83 Sqn
*Andy Hay/www.flyingart.co.uk*

# Torpedo Bombing at Brest

## Kenneth Campbell enrolled straight from the University Air Squadron and sunk several enemy vessels before falling to anti-aircraft artillery.

Born in Ayrshire on April 21, 1917 and educated at Sedbergh School, Kenneth Campbell moved south to Cambridge University in 1935 to study Chemistry at Clare College. It was here that he learned to fly as a graduate of the Cambridge University Air Squadron.

At the outbreak of war in September 1939 Kenneth was mobilised for RAF service and after further training was awarded the rank of Flying Officer. In September 1940 he was allocated to 22 Sqn, flying the Bristol Beaufort torpedo bomber.

His first victory came in March 1941 when he successfully torpedoed a merchant vessel near Borkum in Northern Germany but just days later his aircraft was badly damaged by a pair of Messerschmitt Bf110 twin-engined fighters. Despite extensive damage to his aircraft he landed safely and two days later he torpedoed another vessel, off Ijmuiden in the Netherlands during a 'Rover' patrol.

F/O Campbell was awarded his VC for action over the harbour in Brest, France on April 6, 1941 during an attack on the German battleship *Gneisenau*.

Flying Beaufort N1016 – coded OA-X – Campbell was joined on the mission by navigator Sgt J P Scott DFM (RCAF), wireless operator Sgt R W Hillman and air gunner Sgt W C Mulliss and launched from RAF St Eval, Cornwall.

In order to damage the *Gneisenau* Campbell needed to drop his single torpedo with absolute precision as the ship was moored just 500ft (460m) away from a defensive mole in Brest's inner harbour.

He therefore had to launch his

**Kenneth Campbell VC
(April 21, 1917 –April 6, 1941)**

weapon close to the side of the mole – at a height of just 50ft (15m) – to stand a chance of hitting the ship. However, around 1,000 anti-aircraft weapons of varying calibres surrounded the harbour and the Beaufort was forced to run the gauntlet before reaching its target.

Despite the enormous odds against success Campbell's courage, determination and skill resulted in the torpedo scoring a direct hit and the *Gneisenau* was severely damaged below the waterline.

It was normal for torpedo bombers to escape after an attack by flying at low-level, at full throttle whilst taking erratic evading action, however the terrain at Brest meant this was not possible. Rising ground surrounding the harbour forced Campbell into a steep banking turn, revealing the Beaufort's profile silhouette to the gunners. The aircraft was hit and crashed before it had even left the harbour.

The Germans buried Campbell and his three crewmates with full military honours but his valour was only recognised when the French Resistance managed to relay news of his bravery to Britain. His VC citation was therefore not published until almost a year later on March 13, 1942.

◄ **The Bristol Type 152 Beaufort was a twin-engined torpedo bomber developed with the benefit of the experience gained designing and building the earlier Blenheim light bomber. More than 1,800 were built in the UK and Australia**

**Campbell's Beaufort was registered N1016 and wore the code OA-X of 22 Sqn.** *Andy Hay/www.flyingart.co.uk*

# Bravery in a Blenheim

## From an impoverished background Hughie Edwards would go on to become an Air Commodore and, later, Governor of Western Australia. But he's best remembered for his bravery in a Blenheim.

Hughie Idwal Edwards was the third of five children born to Welsh parents who had emigrated to Fremantle, Western Australia in 1909.

Born on August 1, 1914 Edwards was educated until the age of 14 but forced to leave school when the family could no longer afford to educate him. Described as a "shy, under-confident, introspective and imaginative lad", Edwards found jobs as a shipping office clerk then a stable hand before spending stints in various factories.

He eventually saw the military as his route out of dead-end drudgery and joined the Australian Army in March 1934. A year later he was selected for flying training with the Royal Australian Air Force (RAAF) after which he transferred to the RAF, being granted a short service commission as a Pilot Officer on August 21, 1936.

Upon his arrival in Britain Edwards was allocated to 90 Sqn, flying Bristol Blenheims and was promoted to Flying Officer in May 1938. In the August he was involved in an accident when his Blenheim suffered icing in a storm and he was forced to bale out. However his parachute became entangled in the aircraft as he jumped and he suffered extensive head injuries and a badly broken leg in the subsequent fall.

Air Commodore Sir Hughie Idwal Edwards, VC, KCMG, CB, DSO, OBE, DFC (August 1, 1914 – August 5, 1982)

Surgeons saved Edwards' leg, but it was several inches shorter than his 'good' leg for the rest of his life.

After the accident, he was declared unfit for flying duties until April 1940, when the outbreak of war meant he was needed more than ever and he was posted to 139 Sqn and then 105 Sqn

and promoted to Flight Lieutenant.

On June 15, Edwards – by now an acting Wing Commander – led six Blenheims on a mission looking for enemy shipping anchored near The Hague. He launched a low-level attack on eight merchant vessels and his bombs struck a 4,000-tonne ship earning him the Distinguished Flying Cross (DFC) for his actions.

Less than a month later on July 4 Edwards was the lead aircraft in Operation *Wreckage*; a daylight attack by Blenheims against the port of Bremen, one of the most heavily defended towns in Germany. At 5.21am the flight of 12 bombers took off from RAF Swanton Morley, Norfolk, flying in to attack from a height of just 50ft (15m) whilst dodging telephone wires, high voltage power lines and barrage balloons and evading anti-aircraft fire over the port. Intense fire resulted in the loss of four aircraft but Edwards brought his remaining aircraft safely back, although all had been struck and his own Blenheim IV V6028 – coded GB-D, had been hit more than 20 times. Edwards was awarded the Victoria Cross for his bravery.

In October 1941 Edwards was selected to accompany a group of distinguished RAF commanders under the leadership of Air Vice Marshall

Edwards with his wife, left, and mother-in-law, right, leaving Buckingham Palace after attending his VC investiture ceremony

The Blenheim IV was a development of the earlier aircraft with a longer nose to accommodate a bombardier

This ex-RCAF Bristol Bolingbroke was restored to flying condition at Duxford in the 1980s and painted into the markings of Edwards' Blenheim IV V6028/GB-D. The aircraft flew for the first time after lengthy restoration on May 22, 1987 but was written off less than a month later

Edwards' 105 Sqn Blenheim IV was registered V6028 and wore the codes GB-D *Andy Hay/www.flyingart.co.uk*

Arthur Harris on a goodwill mission to the USA, as a specialist in bombing. While touring the Boeing factory in Seattle on December 7, 1941 Edwards was told that Japan had attacked Pearl Harbor. Before returning to Britain he insisted on visiting Canada where he toured as many training stations as possible to meet young crews.

Later in the war Edwards would relocate with 105 Sqn to Malta in order to conduct operations against Axis shipping carrying reinforcements from Italy to Tripoli and Benghazi.

Upon returning to Britain in 1942, Edwards – by now a Wing Commander – participated in a daylight bombing raid on the Philips Factory at Eindhoven,

the Netherlands for which he received the Distinguished Service Order (DSO); becoming the first airman to receive the VC, DSO and DFC during World War Two.

Edwards became a Group Captain in 1943 but continued to fly operational missions, firstly in Europe and then in the Pacific theatre where he served as Group caption, Head of Bomber Operations in Ceylon.

He would remain in South East Asia Command beyond the end of hostilities serving in places as diverse as Malaya and Kuala Lumpur. Edwards would ultimately receive the Order of the British Empire (OBE) for his services in South-East Asia and would continue to serve

overseas when he was appointed as Station Commander at RAF Habbaniya in Iraq during the Suez Crisis of 1956 and the Iraqi Revolution of 1958.

He finally retired in 1963 having been promoted to Air Commodore. He eventually returned to his native Australia where he was knighted and became Governor of Western Australia in 1974.

Air Commodore Sir Hughie Edwards passed away on August 15, 1982 while on his way to attend a Test Match at the Sydney Cricket Ground. He had enjoyed a full and varied life that he could not have imagined when he left school at 14 as a "shy, under-confident, introspective and imaginative lad." ❖

# The Wing Walking VC

## Sergeant Pilot James Ward was forced to climb out of his Wellington and 'walk' along the wing to put out a fire – actions that saved the crew and earned him a VC

James Allen Ward was born in Wanganui, New Zealand on June 14, 1919 and initially qualified as a teacher before enlisting in the Royal New Zealand Air Force (RNZAF) on July 2, 1940.

After training as a pilot at Taieri and Wigram air bases, Ward sailed to Britain on HMS *Aorangi* in January 1941 before joining the RAF and being allocated to 20 OTU at Lossiemouth, Scotland.

From there Ward was assigned to 75 (NZ) Sqn at RAF Feltwell, Norfolk flying the Vickers Wellington bomber. On the completion of training he was declared operational and promoted to the rank of Sergeant Pilot.

On July 7, 1941 he was flying as second pilot on Wellington IC L7818 – coded AA-R – on a night mission to Münster, Germany. The mission was a success but while returning to base at 13,000ft (3,962m) the bomber was attacked from underneath in the vicinity of Zuiderzee near the Dutch coast. A Luftwaffe Messerschmitt Bf 110 riddled the Wellington with cannon shells and incendiary bullets, injuring the rear gunner. Bravely, the wounded man managed to shoot down the fighter and it was seen to spiral away.

However, fire soon broke out in the Wellington's starboard engine and fuel from a split pipe ignited most of the

**James Allen Ward VC (June 14 1919 – September 15, 1941)**

**Ward standing in the cockpit of Wellington L7818 at Feltwell in July 1941**

wing. The crew cut a hole in the fabric covering on the side of the fuselage and used both fire extinguishers and even the coffee from their flasks to try to extinguish the flames.

As the crew readied themselves to bale out, Ward decided to attempt to smother the fire with an engine cover

and climbed out onto the wing through the damaged astrodome. The pilot slowed the aircraft as much as possible and with a rope tied around his waist Ward began to make his way along the wing, cutting the fabric with an axe to make hand and foot holds where necessary.

**James Ward's Wellington IC was registered L7818 and wore the 75 (NZ) Sqn codes AA-R**
*Andy Hay/www.flyingart.co.uk*

A total of 11,462 Vickers Wellingtons were built for the RAF – more than any other bomber. The Wellington was widely used as a night bomber in the early years of the war but was mostly superseded by the larger four-engined 'heavies by 1943. However, Wellingtons continued to serve throughout the war in other duties, particularly as anti-submarine aircraft

Lying close to the flames he tried to smother the fire but the airflow ripped the fabric engine cover from his hands and it was lost. Ward was now exhausted but he managed to return to the aircraft, by which time the risk of fire was subsiding as most of the fabric around the split petrol pipe had burned itself out. His crawl back over the wing, in which he had previously torn holes, was more dangerous than the outward journey but he succeeded with the help of the aircraft's navigator.

The crew managed to return safely to England and made an emergency landing at Newmarket, Suffolk.

There was initially some reticence to put Ward forward for a VC as his actions had some aspect of self-preservation. Nonetheless, the decision was made and the award was announced on August 5.

Tragically, James Ward was killed in action on September 15, 1941 before he could collect his Victoria Cross. The award was presented to his parents on October 16, 1942. ❖

Wellington L7818 pictured on its return from the Münster raid on July 7, 1941. Visible are the holes Sgt Ward made to help him climb across the wing

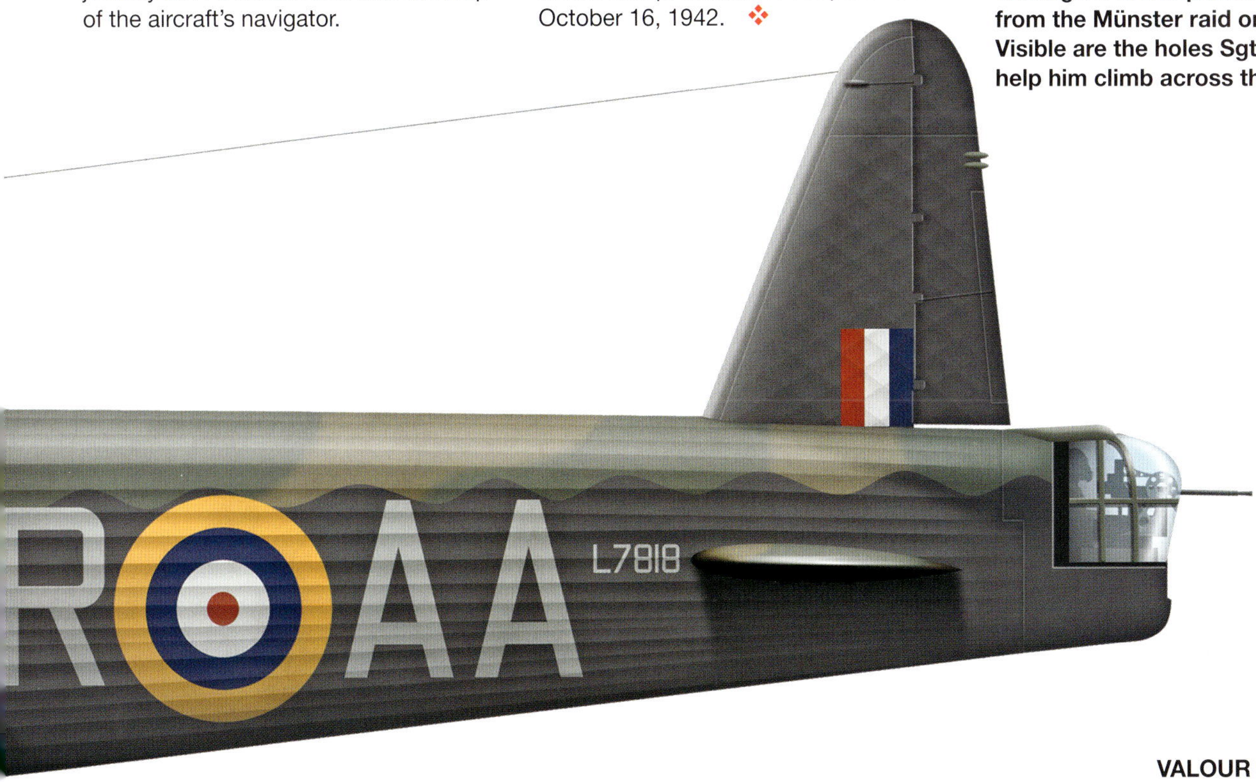

L7818

# The 'Unknown' VC

## Although Arthur Scarf lost his life in action in 1941 it would be 1946 before his heroism was finally noted

Arthur Stewart King Scarf – known to his family as 'John' – was a London boy; born in Wimbledon on June 14, 1913 and educated at the local Kings College.

After graduation, in 1930, he joined an insurance company as an office clerk but described the atmosphere as "suffocating" and almost immediately applied to join the Royal Navy.

His lack of formal qualifications led to him being rejected and after returning to 'Civvy Street' he eventually applied to join the RAF in January 1936 and was accepted for pilot training.

Upon award of his pilot's licence in October 1936 Scarf was briefly posted to 9 Sqn at RAF Scampton, Lincolnshire to fly the ageing Handley Page Heyford before moving to RAF Hemswell, Lincolnshire to fly the equally archaic Hawker Hind with 61 Sqn.

Finally, with war imminent, Scarf got his chance to fly modern aircraft when he joined 62 Sqn at RAF Cranfield, Bedfordshire to fly the Bristol Blenheim I. In mid-1939 the squadron was ordered abroad and Scarf flew his 'personal' Blenheim (L1258/JO-B) to Malaya.

From late 1941 62 Sqn began to see extensive action with Japanese forces. By now Scarf was 28 years old and had been promoted to Squadron Leader.

On December 9, 1941 Scarf set off on a raid on Japanese forces occupying Singora and Patani airfields. An earlier sortie had seen half the attacking Blenheims lost to enemy fighters.

Just before 5.00pm Scarf lined up on the runway at RAF Butterworth as the lead aircraft for a flight of six bombers

**Arthur Stewart King Scarf VC (June 14, 1913 – December 9, 1941)**

– he was flying Blenheim I L1134 – thought to have been coded either PT-F or FX-F.

Scarf and his crew launched just as a wave of Japanese bombers began to bomb the airfield and the rest of the Blenheims were damaged on the ground before they could get airborne.

Angered and frustrated by what he had just witnessed, Scarf elected to carry on his sortie alone and set course for the Siam border with mid-upper gunner Flight Sgt Cyril Rich using his solitary gun to ward off enemy fighters.

With the Blenheim now riddled with bullet holes, a fresh unit of fighters began attacking as the crew neared Singora, but Scarf maintained a steady

course and dropped his bombs on target.

Almost immediately the Blenheim was jumped upon by a dozen Japanese aircraft and Scarf descended to treetop height in an attempt to evade them as Rich used 17 whole drums of ammunition to fend off the fighters,

By the time they reached Allied lines, Scarf had been grievously wounded, including a shattered left arm (he was left handed) and wounds to his lower back. Soon he was slumped semi-conscious over the controls and navigator Flight Sgt Freddie 'Paddy' Calder had to hold him upright in his seat so that he could continue to fly the aeroplane.

Despite drifting in and out of consciousness Scarf was able to successfully crash land the Blenheim at Alor Star airstrip; coming to a rest just 100 yards (91m) from the base hospital where his young wife, Elizabeth, happened to be a nurse. He died two hours later from his injuries, despite his wife donating pints of her own blood. It would be June 30, 1946 before Scarf would be posthumously awarded with the VC for his actions that day. His wife collected the medal from Buckingham Palace on July 30 that year.

The two other crewmen from Scarf's Blenheim were also given awards after the war for their courage during this action; 'Paddy' Calder was awarded a Distinguished Flying Medal and Sgt Cyril Rich (KIA in 1943) received a posthumous Mention in Despatches.

It begs the question as to how many other acts of immense bravery went unrecorded during the bedlam of war. ❖

◄ **With war imminent, Scarf got his chance to fly modern aircraft when he joined 62 Sqn at RAF Cranfield, Bedfordshire to fly the Bristol Blenheim I**

▲ The Bristol Blenheim light bomber was used extensively in the first two years of war and was developed from the Bristol Type 142 commercial aircraft

◄ The Blenheim was one of the first British aircraft to feature an all-metal stressed-skin construction, retractable landing gear, flaps, a powered gun turret and variable-pitch propellers.

▼ The Blenheim Scarf was flying on the mission that earned him the VC was registered L1134 and is thought to have been coded either **PT-F or FX-F** *Andy Hay/ www.flyingart.co.uk*

# Biplanes Against the German Fleet

## Eugene Esmonde led an almost suicidal mission against heavily armed German battleships flying slow, under-armed and out-dated Swordfish biplanes

Eugene Kingsmill Esmonde was a doctor's son born in Thurgoland, Yorkshire on March 1, 1909, but as a young boy he returned to his family's ancestral home in Ireland. The Esmonde baronets were well known in Ireland and Eugene's great uncle, Thomas Esmonde, had been awarded the VC for his bravery during the Crimean War.

Eugene spent his formative years at the imposing family home above Lough Derg, in Drominagh, County Tipperary before being educated at both Wimbledon College in London and Clongowes Wood College in County Kildare, Ireland.

Having been declined for a position as a Catholic missionary priest Esmonde applied for Short Service Commission (SSC) with the RAF in December 1928 and served with 43 Sqn during the early 1930s before being briefly transferred to the Fleet Air Arm (FAA). At the end of his SSC he joined Imperial Airways as a pilot flying long-haul sectors in land and seaplanes.

At the outbreak of war he re-joined the FAA as a Lieutenant Commander (Lt Cdr), by which time he had already amassed around 6,500 flying hours. He was quickly appointed commander of 754 Sqn and by May 1939 was in charge of 825 Sqn aboard HMS *Kestrel* flying the Fairey Swordfish. In July 1940 the unit moved to HMS *Furious* and Esmonde saw extensive service throughout the following year prior to transferring to HMS *Victorious* in the spring of 1941.

On the night of May 23/24 Esmonde led a nine-ship of 825 Sqn Swordfish in a daring attack on the German battleship Bismark. One of the aircraft hit the ship's rudder and it was sunk a few days later

**Eugene Kingsmill Esmonde, VC, DSO (March 1, 1909 –February 12, 1942)**

by Swordfish from HMS *Ark Royal*. For his role in the initial attack Esmonde was awarded the Distinguished Service Order (DSO).

In November 1941, 825 Sqn was deployed aboard HMS *Ark Royal* when she was torpedoed and sank. Esmonde was among the Swordfish pilots to use his aircraft to ferry crewmembers off the stricken vessel – action that resulted in him being Mentioned in Despatches.

However, on February 12, 1942 Esmonde's luck was to finally run out during action against German shipping involved in the 'Channel Dash' (Operation *Cerberus*). The fleet was sailing from Brest and attempting to return to its home bases at Wilhelmshaven and Kiel when 32-year-old Esmonde led a detachment of six Swordfish in an attack on the battlecruisers *Scharnhorst* and *Gneisenau* as well as the heavy cruiser *Prinz Eugen*.

The squadron was operating from RAF Manston, Kent at the time and they knew the fleet was coming. The plan was to launch an attack – codenamed Operation *Fuller* – during cover of darkness but early that morning the ships suddenly appeared in broad daylight. If 825 Sqn waited until darkness their lumbering biplanes would be afforded some element of surprise and defence but it was now evident that the ships would be long gone by nightfall. They had to press home the attack as soon as possible – but the crews knew it would be almost suicidal in daylight.

The RAF's 11 Group offered an escort of ten Spitfires from 72 Sqn and this convinced Esmonde that the mission was 'do-able.' He was to head up a flight of six Swordfish that would attack in two waves of three with the Spitfires providing fighter cover.

▶ **Lt Cdr Eugene Esmonde (second from left) poses with other officers and ratings that were decorated for the part they played in the sinking of the Bismark in October 1941. From left to right are Lt P D Gick (awarded the DSC), Lt Cdr Eugene Esmonde (awarded the DSO), Sub Lt V K Norfolk (awarded the DSC), Pilot Officer L D Sayer (awarded the DSM) and Leading Airman A L Johnson (awarded the DSM).**

A Swordfish drops a 'fish' during a training sortie. The aircraft was out-dated even before the start of the war but continued to operate operationally until May 1945

Esmonde's 823 Sqn Swordfish I was registered W5984 and carried the fuselage code 'H' *Andy Hay/www.flyingart.co.uk*

Esmonde would fly Swordfish W5984 – coded H – and was joined in the open cockpit by observer Lt W H Williams and air gunner Airman W J Clinton. However, as they lined up on the runway at 12.25pm there was no sign of the fighter escorts and with the weather deteriorating the crew were left with no option but to go it alone.

Carrying just a single torpedo each and armed with a single hand-operated Lewis gun in the rear cockpit, the Swordfish were woefully under-armed compared to the battleships and the expected Messerschmitt Bf 109 and Focke-Wulf Fw190 fighters.

The fleet was now just just 23 miles (37km) away in the English Channel and Esmonde led his men into battle. They met the first German fighters ten miles out to sea and and their guns ripped into the fabric-covered biplanes with

ease – yet the crew continued on their track and soon the ships were in sight.

Esmonde elected to target the Scharnhorst and aimed directly towards the bombardment of anti-aircraft fire erupting from the deck. Almost immediately W5984 was hit by a large calibre shell that ripped through the port lower wing. The aircraft was quickly ablaze but Esmonde pressed on his attack, maintaining his course until he was just 3,000 yards (2,743m) from the fleet. This was still outside the normal torpedoing range but Esmonde was seen to be preparing his weapon when the Swordfish became engulfed in flame and crashed into the sea amidst a hail of enemy fire. He is thought to have ultimately succumbed to an attack by an Fw 190.

The other two aircraft in the lead wave – W5983 'G' flown by Sub Lt

Edgar Rose and W5907 'L' flown by Sub Lt C M Kingsmill – pressed home their attacks and successfully launched their weapons before ditching into the sea, too damaged to return to base. The fate of the second wave of three aircraft remains unknown to this day.

There were just five survivors from the 18 men to launch that day, and Sub Lt Rose was the only one to be uninjured. The four surviving officers received the DSO and the enlisted survivor was awarded the Conspicuous Gallantry Medal. Lt Cdr Esmonde was justifiably awarded the VC for his action.

Seven weeks later Lt Cdr Esmonde's body, still in his lifejacket, was washed ashore in the Thames Estuary near the River Medway. He was buried in the Woodlands Cemetery, Gillingham, Kent on April 30, 1942. ❖

# Long Distance Bomber

## John Nettleton was awarded the VC for leading an attack on the MAN diesel engine factory at Augsburg, Southern Germany, 1,000 miles away from his Lincolnshire base

John Dering Nettleton was born in Nongoma, Natal Province, South Africa on June 28, 1917 and educated in Cape Town before joining in the South African Merchant Marine. After 18 months at sea he took up civil engineering working for Cape Town's city council.

It was during a holiday to England in 1938 that Nettleton decided to join the RAF and he was commissioned on December 14 prior to joining various training units for pilot instruction.

In July 1939 he was posted to 207 Sqn at Cottesmore, Rutland but by the end of September he had moved to 98 Sqn at Hucknall, Nottinghamshire and in November he transferred to 185 Sqn – back at Cottesmore – to train on the Handley Page Hampden.

It would be mid-1941 before Nettleton would finally be allocated to an operational squadron – by which time he had been promoted from Flying Officer to Flight Lieutenant. He joined 44 (Rhodesia) Sqn at RAF Waddington, Lincolnshire on June 26 and immediately began flying Hampdens on missions over Germany. In July he was upgraded to Squadron Leader status and on Christmas Eve 44 Sqn became the

**John Dering Nettleton VC (June 28, 1917 –July 13, 1943)**

first RAF squadron to receive the Avro Lancaster bomber.

Following the winter weather and a period of training, on April 14 Nettleton was allocated his own Lancaster (L5508 – coded KM-B). Three days later the crew were finally told about the mission they had been practising

for: they would be attacking the MAN diesel engine factory (responsible for the production of half of Germany's U-boat engines) 1,000 miles (1,609km) away at Augsburg, Southern Germany. Furthermore, they would be making the daring attack in broad daylight!

Nettleton would lead a formation of six 44 Sqn aircraft from Waddington, to be joined by six other aircraft from 97 Sqn at nearby RAF Woodhall Spa.

The Lancasters were 'filled to the gunnels' with 2,154 Imp Gal (9,792lit) of fuel and armed with four 1,000lb (453kg) high explosive bombs with 11-second fuses.

Nettleton lifted KM-B from the Waddington runway at 3.12pm on April 17, 1942 followed by six other Lancasters. The 'spare' soon landed back, leaving the lead six aircraft to form up into two tight 'vic' formations.

The 97 Sqn contingent of six Lancasters was led by Sqn Ldr J S Sherwood flying L7573 – coded OF-K – and all 12 aircraft met up over Selsey Bill before descending to just 50ft (15m) to cross the English Channel. Ahead of them 30 Douglas Boston bombers and almost 800 fighters 'softened' targets along the Lancasters' route but as the two

▲ During his training Nettleton served with 185 Sqn at Cottesmore while learning to fly the Handley Page Hampden in November 1939

▶ For a number of years in the 1970s the Battle of Britain Memorial Flight's Avro Lancaster PA474 flew in the markings of the 'Lanc' Nettleton was flying when he received his VC. The aircraft is seen here displaying at low level at Old Warden, Bedfordshire *Richard Cousens via Author*

As their crews sleep Lancaster Is are prepared for the following night's sorties. These are 50 Sqn aircraft at RAF Swinderby in August 1942 with R5689 in the foreground

The BBMF Lancaster, PA474, wearing KM-B codes in the 1970s
*Richard Cousens via Author*

formations approached the French coast, the 97 Sqn aircraft began to fall behind and they made their own way towards the target to form a separate attack.

For much of the outbound route Nettleton and his men met little resistance. Indeed, as they approached Beaumont le Roger airfield in France, Messerschmitt Bf 109s and Focke-Wulf FW 190s were seen to be landing, having launched to meet the diversionary Bostons. However, the unescorted Lancasters were spotted and the fighters climbed back to press home an attack – within minutes four of the British aircraft had crashed in flames.

By now just Nettleton and F/O Garwell DFC in R5510/KM-A were left to attack the factory, and they released their bombs directly on target. Seconds later Garwell's aircraft was hit by the ground defences and only a skilful emergency landing saved the lives of all but three of his crew.

Behind Nettleton the six aircraft from 97 Sqn were just reaching the target and the now alert anti-aircraft gunners plucked various aircraft from the sky as they approached or escaped the area.

Of the 12 aircraft that launched for the mission seven failed to return. Of the 85 men aboard 49 were listed as missing.

Nettleton landed at RAF Squires Gate, near Blackpool, Lancashire just before 1.00am the following morning. He was immediately recommended for the award of the VC and this was approved on April 28.

Tragically, Sqn Ldr John Nettleton was killed on July 13, 1943 while returning from a raid on Turin, Italy. His Lancaster (ED331/KM-Z) is believed to have been shot down by a fighter off the Brest peninsula in France. His body and those of his crew were never recovered and it would be February 23, 1944 until his death was officially announced – ironically the same day that another announcement was made: the birth of the son he never met.

Nettleton's Lancaster B.I was registered R5508 and wore the KM-B codes of 44 Sqn *Andy Hay/www.flyingart.co.uk*

## CITATION

The announcement and accompanying citation for the decoration was published in supplement to the *London Gazette* on April 28, 1942. It read:

"The KING has been graciously pleased to approve the grant of the VICTORIA CROSS, for valour and resolution in action against the Enemy, to:

"Sqn Ldr John Dering Nettleton - RAF

"Sqn Ldr Nettleton was the leader of one of two formations of six Lancaster heavy bombers detailed to deliver a low-level attack in daylight on the diesel engine factory at Augsburg in Southern Germany on

April 17, 1942. The enterprise was daring, the target of high military importance. To reach it and get back, some 1,000 miles had to be flown over hostile territory.

"Soon after crossing into enemy territory his formation was engaged by 25 to 30 fighters. A running fight ensued. His rear guns went out of action. One by one the aircraft of his formation were shot down until in the end only his own and one other remained. The fighters were shaken off but the target was still far distant. There was formidable resistance to be faced.

"With great spirit and almost defenceless, he held his two remaining aircraft on their perilous course and after a long and arduous

flight, mostly at only 50ft above the ground, he brought them to Augsburg. Here anti-aircraft fire of great intensity and accuracy was encountered. The two aircraft came low over the roof tops. Though fired at from point blank range, they stayed the course to drop their bombs true on the target. The second aircraft, hit by flak, burst into flames and crash-landed. The leading aircraft, though riddled with holes, flew safely back to base, the only one of the six to return.

"Sqn Ldr Nettleton, who has successfully undertaken many other hazardous operations, displayed unflinching determination as well as leadership and valour of the highest order."

# Heroism in 'D for Dog'

**Leslie Manser sacrificed his own life to save those of his crew when their Manchester was hit during a '1,000 bomber' raid on Cologne.**

Although Leslie Thomas Manser was born in New Delhi, India on May 11, 1922 he moved back to Britain as a boy when his father's employment as an engineer in the nation came to an end

Determined to join up and 'do his bit' for the war effort, in 1940 he applied to join the RAF and was enlisted as a pilot trainee in August of the same year.

Upon graduating as a Pilot Officer in May 1941 he was posted to 14 OTU at RAF Cottesmore, Rutland to convert onto the Handley Page Hampden. In August he joined 50 Sqn at RAF Swinderby, Lincolnshire and flew his first operational sortie on August 29.

Manser flew six more sorties over the next eight weeks before returning to 14 OTU as an instructor. However, he was keen to return to an operational squadron and in March 1942 he was posted to 420 Sqn at RAF Waddington, Lincolnshire – again flying Hampdens. The following month he transferred to 50 Sqn, which was based at RAF Skellingthorpe, Lincolnshire and in the throes of trading its Hampdens in for new Avro Manchesters.

On April 8, Manser took part in the squadron's first operational Manchester mission, dropping propaganda over Paris, and then flew a further five missions. On May 6 he was promoted to the rank of Flying Officer.

On the night of May 30/31, 1942 the squadron was to form part of a '1,000-bomber' raid on Cologne and Manser was detailed to ferry Manchester L7301/'D for Dog' from RAF Coningsby, Lincolnshire to Sekellingthorpe in case it

**Leslie Thomas Manser VC
(May 11, 1922 – May 31, 1942)**

was needed as a reserve for the sortie. As it happened both Manser and 'D for Dog' were pressed into action and the aircraft was loaded with 1,260 4lb (1.8kg) incendiary bombs prior to taking off at 11.01pm.

However, his aircraft soon proved to be aptly named. The Manchester should have had an operational ceiling of 18,000ft (5,486m) but 'D for Dog' struggled to reach 7,000ft (2,134m) before its Vulture engines began to overheat.

Undeterred, Manser opted to press on with the mission and an hour later he approached Cologne. Despite flying at less than half the height of the rest of the bomber force L7301 was singled out by searchlights but Manser refused

to take avoiding action until bomb aimer F/O Richard Barnes called "bombs gone."

Almost instantly after the bombs had left the aircraft it was hit by a large shell. Rear gunner Sgt B W Naylor was wounded but the rest of the crew were unharmed.

Manser dived away from the flak, levelling out at just 800ft (244m) before trying to climb back to 2,000ft (610m). (610m). By now the port wing was entirely engulfed in fire but, amazingly, it was quickly extinguished. Despite dumping any unnecessary weight the crippled bomber was still losing height and as they passed through 1,000ft (305m) over occupied Belgium, Manser ordered his crew to bale out.

Wireless operator P/O Norman Horsley helped the injured Naylor from the aircraft before the other crew followed him in 'taking to the silk.' Manser refused Co-pilot Sgt Baveystock's offer of assistance to strap him into his parachute and elected to stay with the aircraft to keep it steady until the crew had safely exited.

Baveystock's 'chute didn't open in time but he was miraculously unhurt when he plunged into 5ft of water. Seconds later the Manchester crashed into a dyke and exploded. Manser had sacrificed himself for his crew.

Barnes, who had been injured as his parachute landed, was taken prisoner. However, Baveystock, Horsley, King, Mills and Naylor were all taken in by sympathetic locals and evaded capture. Their testimonies were instrumental in Manser's posthumous award of the VC. ❖

The Avro Manchester was an operational failure because of its under-developed, under-powered and unreliable engines. However, the aircraft was the forerunner of the successful four-engined Avro Lancaster. This is a IA variant, which had two large fins in place of the original three tails used on the Mk I

▲ An early Manchester I complete with ventral fin. This is similar to the aircraft flown by Manser and his crew

▶ A Manchester IA crew pose for the camera before a mission, the aircraft's Vulture engines are clearly visible

Leslie Manser's Avro Manchester I was registered L7301 and wore the 50 Sqn codes ZN-D – D for Dog
*Andy Hay/www.flyingart.co.uk*

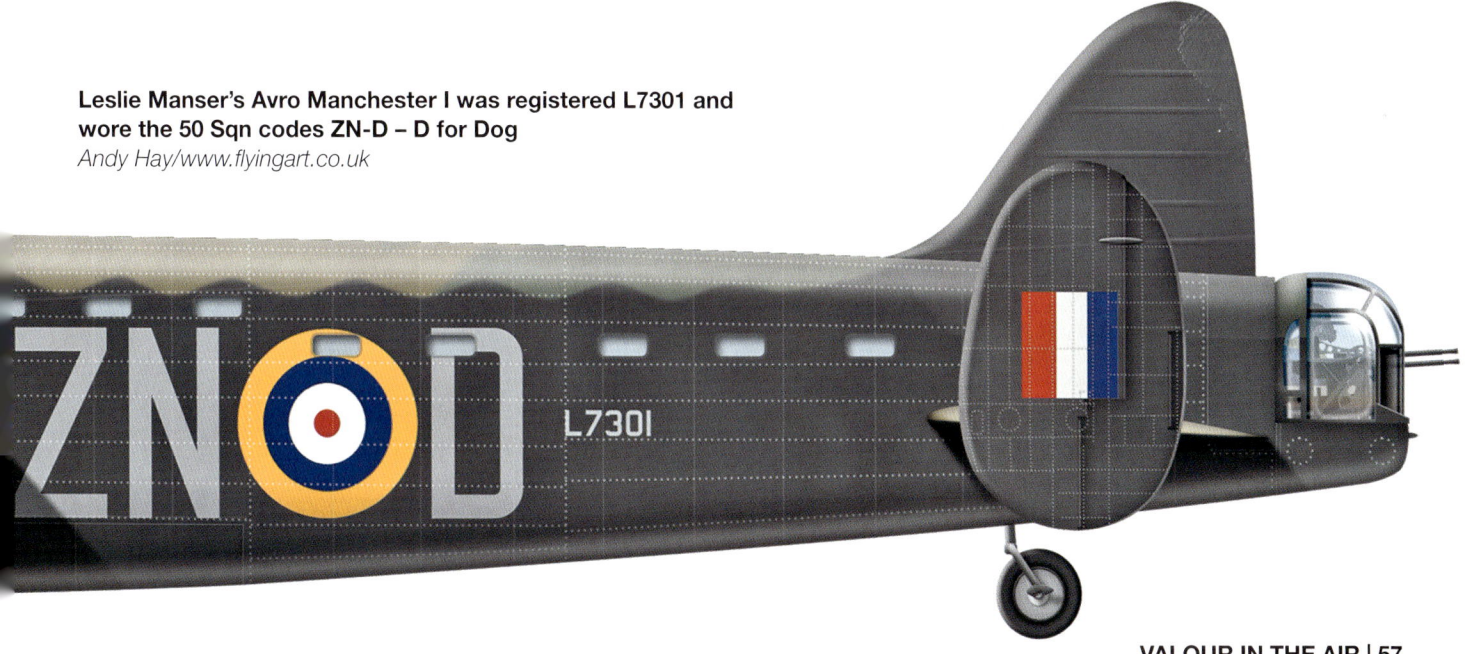

# Stirling Effort

## Despite losing an eye 'Ron' Middleton flew his badly damaged Stirling bomber back from Italy to ensure his crewmates could bale out over friendly territory.

Rawdon Hume Middleton – known to everybody as 'Ron' – was the great-nephew of the colonial explorer Hamilton Hume and was born in Waverley, Sydney, Australia on July 22, 1916.

After graduating from Dubbo High School in New South Wales this athletic young man worked as a jackaroo at Leewang station, the large grazing property his father managed in the state.

However, on October 14, 1940 he enlisted in the Royal Australian Air Force (RAAF) and completed his initial flying training at 5 Elementary Flying Training School (5 EFTS) at Narromine, New South Wales before moving to Canada for advanced training in February 1941. On September 15, 1941 Middleton arrived in Britain where he joined 23 OTU and was promoted to Flight Sergeant and learned to fly the huge Short Stirling four-engined bomber.

On January 1, 1942 he joined 7 Sqn at RAF Oakington, Cambridgeshire – but soon transferred to RAF Waterbeach (also in Cambridgeshire) and then 149 Sqn at RAF Lakenheath, Suffolk where he finally began operational flying over Germany, initially as a second pilot.

On the night of April 6/7 his Stirling was badly damaged by a Messerschmitt

**Rawdon Hume 'Ron' Middleton, VC (July 22, 1916 – November 29, 1942)**

Bf110 night fighter over Essen and suffered an undercarriage collapse on its return to base. It would be July before Middleton was appointed as an aircraft captain, and flew his first raid as a pilot-in-command to Dusseldorf. It was his eleventh operational sortie.

In August Middleton returned to 7 Sqn as part of the newly created

Pathfinder Force. Poor navigation on one of his first sorties with the squadron saw his Stirling over Munich, 100 miles from their intended target and the aircraft ran out of fuel just as it was landing at the diversion field at RAF Manston, Kent on the way home. With no power it ploughed into a number of parked Spitfires and crashed into the station armoury. Luckily nobody was hurt but Middleton was asked to swap his navigator for future missions. He refused to do so and 7 Sqn's boss duly returned him to 149 Sqn for the remainder of his war.

His crew continued to fly missions and on the night of November 28/29, 1942 Middleton flew Stirling BF372 – coded OJ-H – on a sortie to bomb the Fiat aircraft works in Turin, Italy. It was his 29th combat sortie, one short of the 30 required for completion of a 'tour' and mandatory rotation off combat operations. Two of his three air gunners (Sgt John Mackie and Sgt Harold Gough) had already surpassed their 30 sorties required for completion of a 'tour' but elected to stay on to support their 'skipper'.

Also aboard the aircraft was air gunner Sgt Douglas Cameron, second pilot Flt Sgt Leslie Hyder, navigator F/O

**Ron Middleton's Stirling was registered BF372 and wore the 149 Sqn codes of OJ-H**
*Andy Hay/www.flyingart.co.uk*

Stirlings are readied for their next mission

A flight of Short Strlings en route to a target in Germany

George Royde, wireless operator P/O Norman Skinner and flight engineer Sgt James Jeffery.

The Stirling lifted off from Lakenheath at 6.14pm with an 8,000lb (3,629kg) bomb load and full fuel tanks. It soon became apparent that fuel burn was excessive due to stronger than forecast headwinds, the autopilot was inoperative and the aircraft could also not climb above 12,000ft (3,658m). Middleton informed his crew that they would need to navigate 'through' the 15,000ft (4,572m) Alps and it would be touch and go whether they had enough fuel to get home – yet they pressed on.

Having narrowly missed the peaks of the mountains in the moonless sky, the Stirling's crew spotted Turin and began a dive towards the city. Almost instantly they were caught in a hail of anti-aircraft fire.

The port wing was heavily damaged and shrapnel peppered the fuselage before a direct hit was scored on the windscreen. Middleton was grievously wounded and lost consciousness for a few seconds, causing the aircraft to dive steeply to just 800ft before he came around and ordered the bombs to be dropped. Suffering from shrapnel wounds to the arms, legs and body as well as having his right eye torn from its socket and his jaw shattered, Middleton was rapidly losing blood; he was barely able to see and could only breathe with difficulty. Nonetheless he was determined to fly his crippled aircraft home, and return his crew to

Middleton (far right) and classmates from 7 Empire Air Training Scheme course at pose in front of a Tiger Moth at 5 Elementary Flying Training School Narromine in 1940

safety - many of whom were injured themselves.

On the return flight the men threw everything they could overboard in order to lighten the aircraft, even chopping at the structure with axes. Middleton remained in his pilot's seat staring through the shattered windscreen with his one remaining eye.

After four painful hours the Stirling reached the English coast with just five minutes of fuel remaining and Middleton ordered his men to bale out. Five did so and landed safely, but Mackie and Jeffery remained to try to talk Middleton into a forced landing. He continued to refuse and steered the aircraft out over the sea. His two friends finally left the aircraft but Middleton

stayed with the machine until it crashed into the Channel. Mackie and Jeffery did not survive the night in the freezing sea.

Flt Sgt Middleton was posthumously promoted to Pilot Officer and awarded the VC for his valour. His citation noted that his "devotion to duty in the face of overwhelming odds is unsurpassed in the annals of the Royal Air Force."

P/O Royde was awarded a DFC while Flt Sgt Hyder, Flt Sgt Cameron and Sgt Gough were all awarded the Distinguished Flying Medal (DFM).

Coincidentally, Cameron would also be a member of Flt Sgt Ian Willoughby Bazalgette's crew when the Canadian would be awarded a posthumous VC on August 4, 1944 (see page 94) ❖

# Bravery in the Desert

## Hugh Malcolm led a number of daring missions in North Africa in 1942 before he died in a Bristol Blenheim V in Tunisia. These sorties all contributed to the decision to award him a posthumous Victoria Cross

Huge Malcolm was a proud Scot, born in Dundee on May 2, 1917 and educated at Craigflower Preparatory School near Dunfermline and Glenalmond College in Perthshire. He enrolled at Cranwell on January 9, 1936 and graduated as a commissioned pilot in December 1937.

He was assigned to 26 Sqn at RAF Catterick, Yorkshire the same month and after Christmas he was briefly seconded to the School of Army Co-operation at Old Sarum, Wiltshire to learn how to fly the Westland Lysander.

On May 20, 1939 Malcolm's career was almost cut short when he crashed a Lysander while practising for the Empire Air Day flying display at Manchester. He suffered a fractured skull and spent four months in hospital – where he met the nurse who would later become his wife.

Malcolm returned to flying in September 1939 and flew with a variety of Lysander units until he joined 17 OTU in December 1941 to convert onto the Bristol Blenheim IV. He was then posted to 18 Sqn as a Squadron Leader flying from RAF Wattisham, Suffolk until the type was declared obsolete for missions over occupied Europe.

In August 1942 the squadron was re-equipped with 'new' Blenheim Vs and Malcolm was promoted to the rank of Wing Commander. In this capacity he took the unit out to Algeria to support

**Hugh Gordon Malcolm VC (May 2, 1917 – December 4, 1942)**

Operation *Torch*; the Allied invasion of North Africa.

His first mission in the area was a disaster when he led the squadron in a low-level attack on Bizerta, Tunisia without fighter escort. Although they successfully dropped their weapons and also brought down a Junkers Ju-52 and Messerschmitt Bf 109, the squadron was caught in bad weather on the way back to base and two aircraft collided in cloud. Another fell to German fighters.

Undeterred, Malcolm led several

other sorties in the area and on November 28 he again led his squadron against Bizerta airfield. Finally, on December 4, he took off from Souk-el-Arba, Tunisia and led a six-ship formation attack on an enemy airfield near Chougai.

Shortly after landing Malcolm received a request from the Army to attack the same area again immediately. Although no fighter cover could be arranged at short notice – and the enemy would now be on high alert – he agreed and mustered a fleet of eleven Blenheims.

Malcolm was joined in Blenheim V (BA875 - coded W) by his regular navigator P/O J Robb and wireless operator/air gunner P/O James Grant DFC. He led the formation into the skies at 3.15pm – although one aircraft burst a tyre on take-off, reducing the task force to ten. Just minutes later another aircraft crashed due to engine problems, but fortunately the crew escaped without serious injury.

Without fighter support the nine Blenheims flew tight formation so their gunners could defend themselves to best effect. As they approached the enemy airfield, around 50 Luftwaffe Messerschmitt Bf 109 fighters from Gruppen I and Gruppen II of Jagdeschwader 2 launched to meet them over the desert.

**Hugh Malcolm's 18 Sqn Blenheim V was registered BA875 and coded W**
*Andy Hay/ww.flyingart.co.uk*

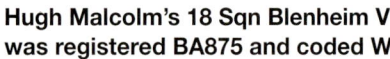

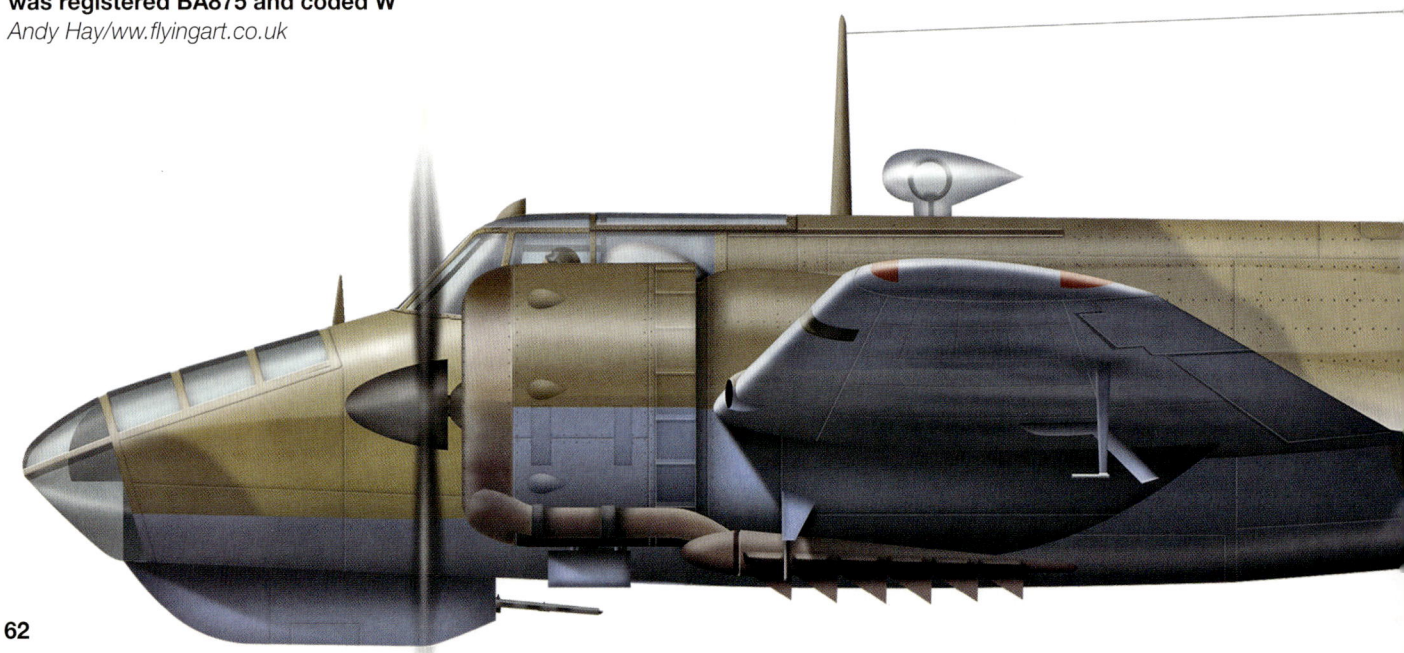

The Blenheim V was also delivered with a glass nose for the conventional bombing role

In the following five minutes the German fighters massacred the under-armed Benheims claiming a total of 12 victories (even though there were only nine aircraft on the scene!).

From the scant evidence available it appears that the final aircraft to be shot down was Hugh Malcolm's BA875 – the Blenheim was reported to have been seen crashing in flames some 15 miles west of the target. Allied forces arrived on the scene after less than a minute but wcrc only able to drag Robb's body from the airframe before it exploded.

Fittingly, Hugh Malcolm was awarded a posthumous VC on April 27, 1943 for various missions he had commanded in the North Africa campaign. ❖

The final variant of the Blenheim was conceived as an armoured ground attack aircraft, with a solid nose containing four more Browning machine guns. Originally known as the Bisley, the production aircraft were renamed the Blenheim V and featured a strengthened structure, pilot armour, interchangeable nose gun pack or bombardier position

# Australia's Only Pacific VC Winner

**Bill Newton was awarded the Victoria Cross for his actions flying Douglas Boston bombers. He was the only Australian airman to earn the decoration in the Pacific theatre and the only one to do so flying with an RAAF squadron.**

Born in Melbourne, Australia on June 8, 1919 William Ellis 'Bill' Newton became a member of the Cadet Corps during his schooling and joined the Citizens Military Force in 1938, serving as a private in the machine-gun section of the Royal Melbourne Regiment.

At the outbreak of World War Two, he immediately enlisted and joined the Royal Australian Air Force (RAAF). After elementary, basic and advanced flying training in Australia he was earmarked as ideal instructor material and prevented from joining a frontline squadron. It would be May 9, 1942 before Newton finally realised his ambition and was posted to 22 Sqn RAAF to fly Douglas Boston attack bombers. By now he had

▼ The DB-7C Bostons were destined for the Dutch East Indies Air Force, but the Japanese victory in the East Indies was complete before they were delivered. Part of this order was stranded in Australia so 31 were assembled at Richmond Air Base in New South Wales and flown by the RAAF's 22 Sqn. The assembly and operation of these bombers was hampered by the fact that their manuals and instrument panels were printed in Dutch

been promoted to the rank of Flight Lieutenant.

In addition to maintenance issues the Bostons had originally been produced for the Dutch East Indies Air Force so the manuals and handbooks were all written in Dutch. Eventually the air and ground crews got used to the new type and on November 7 they were flown from the OTU in Victoria to Port Morseby in New Guinea where they operated alongside RAAF Bristol Beaufighters.

Newton undertook the first of his 52 sorties against Japanese forces on January 1, 1943 and the squadron soon specialised in low-level missions through the hazardous mountain terrain. Newton would go on to take an active role in the Battle of the Bismarck Sea, gaining a reputation for diving straight at his targets without making evasive manoeuvres.

On March 16, Newton led a sortie against Japanese forces in the town of Salamaua in Papua New Guinea flying Boston A28-15. The aircraft was badly damaged approaching the target but Newton continued with the mission and dropped his bombs at low level on buildings, ammunition dumps and fuel stores; even returning for a second pass to strafe the target with machine-gun fire.

**William Ellis Newton, VC
(June 8, 1919 – March 29, 1943)**

Nursing the crippled aircraft back to base, Newton's actions that day led his squadron commander to make out a recommendation for him to be awarded the Victoria Cross, but yet more bravery was still to come.

On March 18 Newton was aloft again, this time flying A28-3 – coded DU-Y – against the familiar targets in Salamaua.

**Bill Newton's Boston was registered A28-3 and wore 22 Sqn RAAF codes as DU-Y**
*Andy Hay/www.flyingart.co.uk*

**Douglas Bostons of 22 Sqn RAAF head out on patrol over the South Pacific in 1943**

Joining him in the bomber were his usual navigator (Sgt Basil Eastwood) and wireless operator/gunner (Flt Sgt John Lyon) and as the crew swept in towards the town at just 50ft (15m) an anti-aircraft battery opened fire on the Boston. They scored several direct hits and the port engine quickly caught fire causing Newton to break off his attack.

Other attacking aircraft noted the Boston ditching in the sea adjacent to the coast with two crewmembers seen swimming ashore. These were later identified as Newton and Lyon; Eastwood was presumed drowned or to have already been killed.

The survivors were quickly captured by the Japanese and interrogated. Ten days later Lyon was executed by being bayonetted in the back and Newton was taken back to Salamaua and handed over to his original captors. On March 29, as the sun was setting, Newton was bound and forced to kneel before Sub-Lieutenant Uichi Komai (the naval officer who had captured him). Komai drew his sword and beheaded the prisoner with a single blow.

At the time Newton's posthumous VC was awarded for his actions on March 16–18, he was listed as "missing, presumed dead"; the citation, which incorrectly implied that he was shot down on March 17 rather than the following day, listed him as having failed to escape from his sinking aircraft. Newton's true fate only became known years later when a Japanese soldier's diary was discovered. The Japanese observer described the Newton as "composed" as he faced his execution, and "unshaken to the last". ❖

**Newton poses for the camera in 1942**

# Valour over the Low Countries

## The second of three New Zealand pilots to be awarded the Victoria Cross, Leonard Trent received the accolade for bravery flying a Lockheed Ventura on a Ramrod mission over the occupied Low Countries.

Leonard Henry Trent was born in Nelson, New Zealand on April 14, 1915. He joined the Royal New Zealand Air Force (RNZAF) in 1937 and began to learn to fly at Wigram airfield before graduating to fly the Vickers Vildebeest biplane bomber.

In mid-1938 he was posted to the RAF on exchange, remaining in the British military after the outbreak of war.

In September 1939 Trent went to France as part of XV Sqn, flying Fairey Battles on high-level photo-reconnaissance missions over enemy territory. However, by the end of the year the unit had been withdrawn back to Britain and began to convert onto the Bristol Blenheim IV.

He flew flew various missions over the coming year and in July 1940 Trent was awarded the Distinguished Flying Cross (DFC) for his bravery over Europe.

After a short break to work as a flying instructor Trent returned to operational flying in March 1942, by which time he had been promoted to Squadron Leader and appointed commander of B Flights of 487 (NZ) Sqn. Based at RAF Feltwell, Norfolk, the unit had recently converted onto the Lockheed Ventura for daylight bombing missions over occupied Europe.

An attack on the Royal Dutch Steel Works at Ijmuiden on May 2 by 464 Sqn (also equipped with the Ventura) resulted in only moderate damage so 107 Sqn's Douglas Boston IIIs were tasked to repeat the mission

**Leonard Henry Trent VC DFC (April 14, 1915 –May 19, 1986)**

the following day. Stiff Luftwaffe opposition was expected so 12 crews from 487 (NZ) Sqn were ordered to conduct a diversionary 'Ramrod' low-level attack on the Amsterdam power station.

Sqn Ldr Trent was to fly the lead aircraft (AJ209 – coded EG-V) in the first wave of six Venturas. Joining him were Flt Lt V Philips (navigator), F/O Roy Thomas (wireless operator) and Sgt W Trenery (mid upper gunner) and they lifted off from Methwold just after 4.30pm.

Almost immediately one Ventura (EG-Q flown by Sgt Barker) lost its escape hatch and was forced to turn back, but soon the remainder of the bombers met up with Spitfire escorts from 18, 167 and 504 Sqns and set course for Holland, skimming the waves to stay below German radar. The bombers were supposed to meet more Spitfires (from 122 and 453 Sqns) as they crossed the Dutch coast but the fighters arrived early and, climbing for altitude, they alerted the German radar operators to an imminent attack.

By unfortunate coincidence the German Governor of Holland was visiting the town of Haarlem that day and the Luftwaffe had drafted in extra airpower to defend him.

As the British bombers approached the town, around 70 Focke-Wulf FW-190s and Messerschmitt Bf109s were lying in wait. The fighter onslaught was relentless and soon six Venturas had been lost, leaving just Trent and two other aircraft to press home the attack.

Then, one Bf109 made a fatal mistake and turned in front of Trent's aircraft – the New Zealander immediately pressed the trigger for the two .303 and two .50 machine guns in the nose and the German fighter was shot from the sky. Moments later another Ventura fell out of formation just as the power station came into view.

Undeterred, Trent concentrated on the bombing run and when Phillips called 'Bombs Gone' the crew realised

**A Lockheed Ventura is prepared for another sortie in June 1943**

Trent's Ventura was registered AJ209 and wore the EG-V codes of 487 (NZ) Sqn
*Andy Hay/www.flyingart.co.uk*

The first RAF Venturas started to arrive in Britain in April 1942 and by the end of August that year enough had been ferried over the Atlantic to equip three Squadrons. The type was soon relegated to medium level bombing as it was found to be vulnerable at low level, despite being 43kts faster and carrying more than twice as many bombs as its predecessor, the Hudson

they were the only Ventura left flying. The crew turned for home but it was too late – an enormous explosion rocked the aircraft. The Venture pitched up, stalled and entered an inverted spin. Trent opened the escape hatch just before another violent explosion which ejected him from the aeroplane at a height of around 7,000ft (2,134m).

He floated down and landed in a ploughed field where he was captured by Germans and reunited with Phillips – the only other survivor.

Trent was moved to the Stalag Luft III prison camp for the remainder of the war – albeit with a brief sojourn outside when he was a member of the famed 'Great Escape.' He was liberated from the camp on May 2, 1945 and upon his return to Britain, discovered that his final operational flight had earned him the VC.

Quiet and unassuming, Trent disliked the fuss caused, especially during its investiture at Buckingham Palace on April 12, 1946, and was uncomfortable with the publicity. However, he

continued in the RAF after the war and had the dubious distinction of having to eject from both a de Havilland Vampire and a Gloster Meteor! He later commanded the Vickers Valiant equipped 214 Sqn Squadron and saw further action during the Suez Crisis.

Leonard Trent finished his career as a Group Captain and was ultimately appointed an Air Attaché to Washington DC. He moved to Australia in 1965 and returned to New Zealand in 1977 where he eventually passed away peacefully on May 19, 1986. ❖

# The Dambusting VC

**Perhaps the most famous of all aviating VC holders, Guy Gibson commanded the legendary 617 Sqn during Operation Chastise in May 1943.**

Guy Penrose Gibson was born in Simla, India on August 12, 1918 where his father was working as a civil servant. When the family returned to Britain, Guy entered the public school system.

It has been reported that his love of flying stemmed from a school tutor who owned a retired Great War-era biplane and often took his students for air experience flights.

If so, it made an indelible impression on young Guy who attempted to pursue an aviation career at the earliest opportunity. In 1935, at the age of just 17, Gibson applied to Vickers Aviation for a job as a test pilot but was politely told to join the RAF in order to learn to fly and gain some experience. Initially rejected for being too short, Gibson was eventually accepted by the RAF for a commission on January 31, 1937 – although his aim was still to gain experience before pursuing a civilian career.

Upon graduation in September of the same year he was posted to 83 Sqn at RAF Scampton, Lincolnshire to fly the Hawker Hind biplane bombers. With conflict in Europe now looking ever more likely 83 Sqn traded its ageing equipment in for Bristol Blenheim I monoplanes and Handley Page Hampdens – the first arriving on October 31, 1938.

**Guy Penrose Gibson, VC, DSO & Bar, DFC & Bar**
**(August 12, 1918 – September 19, 1944)**

At the outbreak of war the squadron was put on standby and on September 3, 1939 Guy Gibson flew Hampden L4040 – coded 'C' – as part of the unit's first operational mission. In the event the bombers failed to find the German naval targets they had been tasked with attacking and dropped their bombs in the North Sea before returning to base.

After flying a further 27 operational sorties – and being awarded a DFC on July 8, 1940 – Gibson was finally rested but he was eager to return to the 'sharp end' of the war and requested a new posting. He therefore joined 29 Sqn at RAF West Malling, operating Bristol Beaufighter night fighters, and flew his first sortie on December 10, 1940. He and his crewman, Sgt R H James, would claim three aircraft destroyed, one probable and five damaged before Gibson was transferred to a flying instructor role in December 1941.

Once again he pushed for a return to operational flying and in April 1942 Gibson joined 106 Sqn at RAF Coningsby, Lincolnshire to fly the Avro Manchester and Avro Lancaster. Gibson flew a large number of sorties over the next year and on January 16, 1943 he took the BBC's war correspondent, Richard Dimbleby on a sortie to Berlin. Dimbleby described the raid in a later radio broadcast and Gibson was pleased at the opportunity to communicate what life was like for the aircrews.

In March he made his final flight with the squadron and was summoned to 5 Group HQ and asked to fly one more 'special' mission.

In order to complete the as yet secret mission Gibson was given carte blanche to form his own squadron. The

**At the outbreak of war Gibson was flying Handley Page Hampdens with 83 Sqn and he was awarded a DFC for his duties on July 8, 1940**

An 'Upkeep' bouncing bomb used for the dam busting mission, fitted below Gibson's Lancaster B.III (Special)

Prior to their departure for the Ruhr Dams on May 16, 1943 Gibson (in the door) posed for a publicity photo with his crew. Left to right: Flt Lt R D Trevor-Roper DFM; Sgt J Pulford; Flt Sgt G A Deering RCAF; P/O F M Spafford DFM RAAF; Flt Lt R E G Hutchinson DFC; Wing Commander Guy Gibson and P/O H T Taerum RCAF

**An 'Upkeep' is dropped from a Lancaster during testing in May 1943**

end result was 617 Sqn and Operation *Chastise* would call for Lancasters to fly at extremely low level and drop a Top Secret weapon on hydroelectric dams in Germany's Ruhr Valley.

A total of 20 Lancasters were modified to carry a 9,250lb (4,196kg) cylindrical 'Upkeep' bomb containing 6,600lb (2,994kg) of high explosive. The weapon, designed by Barnes Wallis, was specially created to 'backspin' when it hit the water and bounce along the surface until it met the dam. It would then roll down the damn wall and explode at a depth of 30ft (9.14m). However, to be effective the 'bouncing bomb' had to be dropped within very precise parameters: the aircraft needed to be slower than 217kts (250mph), at exactly 60ft (18.3m) and the weapon needed to be launched between 400-450 yards (365-412m) from the dam wall.

On May 16, 1943, 19 Lancasters launched from RAF Scampton at 9.30pm. At the head of the formation was Wg Cdr Guy Gibson flying ED932/AJ-G, who led his section of nine aircraft towards the Möhne Damn; if they had any weapons leftover they would then proceed to the Eder dam. Meanwhile,

## " Gibson flew his Lancaster slightly ahead to draw the fire away from the attacking aircraft "

five other aircraft routed towards the Sorpe Dam and five more acted as back-up aircraft to be directed by Gibson mid-flight as needed.

Gibson made a dummy run over the dam to assess the defensive weaponry before making his initial attack. However, the bomb was released short and did not damage the dam and it took about five minutes for the water to settle down after the explosion.

He then called in John Hopgood in AJ-M to make his attack but his Lancaster was hit by flak and although the crew managed to launch their weapon before the aircraft exploded the bomb overshot and destroyed an electrical station below the dam.

Gibson called in Sqn Ldr Harold 'Mick' Martin and his crew in AJ-P but this time he opted to fly his own Lancaster slightly ahead to draw the fire away from the attacking aircraft. Again, the weapon failed to find its target.

Martin then flew alongside Sqn Ldr Young's AJ-A to draw the flak

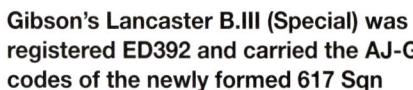

**Gibson's Lancaster B.III (Special) was registered ED392 and carried the AJ-G codes of the newly formed 617 Sqn**
*Andy Hay/www.flyingart.co.uk*

**The Eder Dam; after 617 Sqn's visit on May 16/17, 1943**

while Gibson flew another route to confuse the gunners further. Young dropped his weapon but it was only when the next aircraft began its attack that the crew realised the dam had been breached. At 12.56am Gibson's wireless operator radioed back to base to report the mission had been a success.

The surviving crew departed for home while Gibson and Young flew across to the Eder with the other aircraft to help direct the attack on the Eder dam. At 1.54am Hutchinson radioed home to announce the breaching of the second dam.

Meanwhile members of the back-up formation were attacking the Sorpe dam, which although it was not breached was significantly damaged.

The effect of the mission were felt across the Rhur Valley with 140 million cubic metres of water rushing through the dams and an 18ft (5.5m) high tidal wave extended 24 miles from the target. Around 125 factories and 46 bridges were destroyed or damaged and some 1,294 people and 6,500 cattle were killed.

Off the 19 RAF crews involved in the mission, eight failed to return. The first of the survivors landed back at Scampton at 3.11am and Gibson touched down at 4.15am. Of the eight crews who actually attacked and then returned from the mission 33 men were given gallantry awards and Gibson received the VC for the coordination and leadership of the most famous mission in RAF history.

After a tour of the USA and Canada Gibson returned to Britain and although he was able to 'scrounge' several operational sorties his requests to return to fully active status were resolutely refused. However, in September 1944 AOC Bomber Command Arthur 'Bomber' Harris relented and approved Gibson for "just one more sortie" providing it was against a soft target.

At 7.51pm on September 19 Gibson launched from RAF Woodhall Spa, Lincolnshire flying a 627 Sqn de Havilland Mosquito B.XX (KB267 – coded E) with Sqn Ldr James Warwick DFC as his navigator. They were part of a force of ten Mosquitos and 220 Lancasters attacking industrial targets in Rheydt and Mönchengladbach and the mission was a resounding success. However, Gibson's aircraft failed to return to base and it was later discovered crashed near Steenbergen in the Netherlands. He was just 26 years old when he died. ❖

# Recommended by the Enemy

**Lloyd Trigg's award is unique, as it was awarded on evidence solely provided by the enemy, for an action in which there were no surviving Allied witnesses to corroborate his gallantry.**

New Zealander Lloyd Allan Trigg was born in Houhora, North Island. He enjoyed flying and had originally considered joining the Royal New Zealand Air Force (RNZAF) directly from college but in 1938 he got married and started a family. However, the outbreak of the war in Europe prompted Trigg to finally enlist.

After learning to fly in New Zealand in the summer of 1941 he was sent to Canada for advanced training under the Empire Training Scheme. Trigg graduated in January 1942 and transferred to 31 General Reconnaissance School on Canada's Prince Edward Island for conversion training on the Lockheed Hudson bomber. He sailed for England in October 1942 but his stay was brief as he was quickly allocated to 200 Sqn in North Africa to fly in maritime support of merchant and naval convoys sailing the eastern Atlantic seaboard.

Trigg arrived in theatre on January 1, 1943 and flew his first mission ten days later. By the end of February he'd completed eight more sorties and in early March he successfully depth-charged a German U-boat – the mission earning him a DFC.

In May the squadron began the conversion from Hudsons to the new, large, four-engined Consolidated Liberator. F/O Trigg was sent to the Bahamas for training and returned to North Africa in July – at the height of the rainy season.

The squadron's usual base at Yundum, Gambia was soon waterlogged so the Liberators and their crews

**Lloyd Allan Trigg VC DFC
(May 5, 1914 – August 11, 1943)**

departed to the USAAF base at Rufisque near Dakar, Senegal. It was from here that they performed their first operational Liberator sortie on August 11, with Trigg flying BZ832 – coded 'D'. Joining him was another Liberator flown by W/O 'Rikki' Johnson and the two bombers took off at 7.29am, routing out to sea on what was expected to be a 12-hour anti-submarine mission.

At 9.45am Trigg spotted U-boat U-462 on the surface some 240 miles south west of Dakar. The 500-tonne submarine was on its third patrol of the war and had launched from La Pallice,

France on July 7. Its supply ship had recently been sunk so the 'sub' was heading for home, but now it was firmly in Trigg's sights and just 6,000 yards (5,486m) away.

However, as the Liberator descended and began its lengthy depth charge run, Oberleutnant Klemens Schamong ordered the U-boat's two 20mm cannon to be swung towards the bomber. His crews opened fire and the Liberator was soon ablaze. Undeterred, Trigg pressed on with the attack, maintaining a steady course despite the barrage of anti-aircraft artillery. The Liberator passed over the submarine at a height of just 50ft (15.2m) and dropped six depth charges; two of which exploded close to the hull and caused the U-468 to sink within ten minutes.

Sadly, despite the mission success, BZ832 crashed into the sea and exploded just 300 yards (275m) from the stricken sub. All crew members perished immediately and half of the U-boat's sailors were instantly killed. Just 20 seamen escaped the submarine but several of those were subsequently killed by sharks and barracudas or succumbed to the poisonous gas being emitted by the ship's damaged batteries.

Ultimately just seven sailors, including Commander Schamong, survived the encounter. They were found the following day, drifting in a life raft they'd salvaged from the crashed Liberator, and rescued by the crew of the corvette HMS Clarkia. Under interrogation the Germans revealed the full extent of Trigg's bravery and their testimony resulted in the award of a posthumous Victoria Cross. ❖

**Trigg's 200 Sqn Liberator was registered BZ832 and wore the fuselage code 'D'**
*Andy Hay/www.flyingart.co.uk*

▲ Trigg's early squadron service saw him flying the Lockheed Hudson with 200 Sqn and in February 1943 he was awarded a DFC for successfully depth-charging a German U-boat

◄ In May 1943, 200 Sqn began the conversion from Hudsons to the new, large, four-engined Consolidated Liberator. The RAF used the Liberator in a variety of roles but Coastal Command was by far the most prominent

▼ A Consolidated Liberator GR.IV of Coastal Command

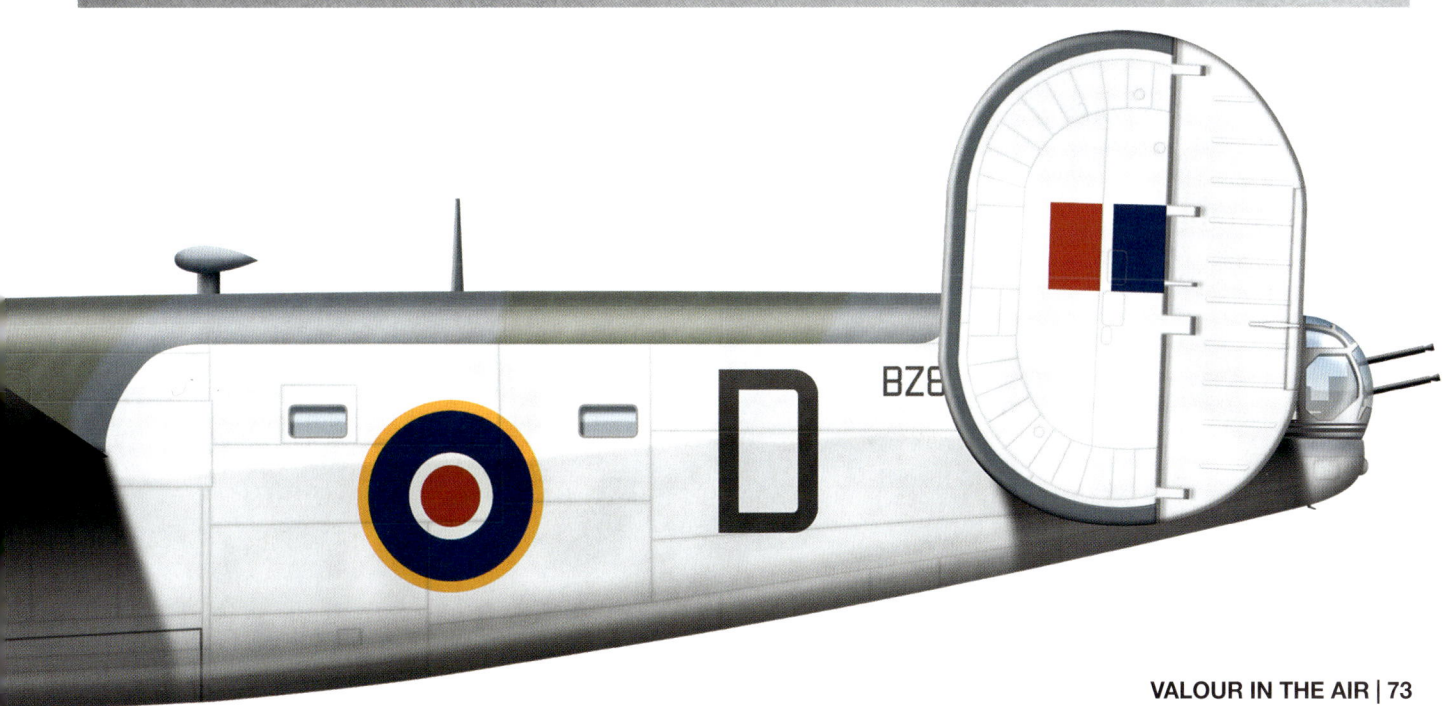

# Highest Praise from 'Bomber' Harris

### Writing to Arthur Aaron's family after his death, Arthur 'Bomber' Harris declared: "In my opinion, never even in the annals of the RAF, has the VC been awarded for skill, determination and courage in the face of the enemy of the highest order than that displayed by your son."

Arthur Louis Aaron was born in Leeds, Yorkshire on March 5, 1922 to a British father and a Swiss mother. It was undoubtedly his mother's influence that led him to a lifelong interest in mountains and mountaineering but his love of flying stemmed from a flight with the legendary Alan Cobham Flying Circus when it visited Penrith in the 1930s.

At the end of his schooling 'Art' Aaron enrolled at Leeds College of Architecture in 1939 and immediately joined the Leeds University Air Squadron. In 1941 he enlisted in the RAF and was sent to the USA where he completed his advanced flying training with No 1 (British) FTS at Terrell, Texas before graduating as a Sergeant pilot in June 1942.

Upon his return to Britain he was assigned to 1657 Heavy Conversion Unit to learn how to fly the giant Short Stirling bomber and on April 17, 1943 he was assigned to 218 Sqn at RAF Downham Market, Norfolk.

Over the next three months Aaron and his regular crew flew 20 operational sorties and he insisted that 'his' men all learned how to fly and fight in every position in the aircraft in case they were ever needed to do so in an emergency. On one mission Aaron successfully brought his aircraft home despite suffering extensive flak damage; flying that earned him a Distinguished Flying Medal (DFM).

On August 12, 1943 Aaron and his colleagues climbed into Stirling EF452 – coded HA-O – and launched on their 21st mission. The target was Turin, Italy and aboard the bomber that day were Sgt Cornelius 'Bill' Brennan (navigator), Flt Sgt Allan Larden (bomb aimer), Sgt T 'Jimmy' Guy (wireless operator), Sgt Malcolm Mitchem (flight engineer), Sgt J Richmond (upper gunner), Sgt Thomas McCabe (rear gunner) along with Flt Sgt Arthur 'Art' Aaron as the aircraft commander.

As they crossed the French coast at 10,000ft (3,048m) Aaron continued to coax the heavily laden bomber even higher and had eventually reached 14,000ft (4,267m) by the time they reached the Alps. As he looked out at

**Arthur Louis Aaron VC, DFM (March 5, 1922 –August 13, 1943)**

Mont Blanc, bathed in moonlight, the keen mountaineer is reported to have told his crewmembers of his desire to climb the summit – which was still nearly 2,000ft (609m) higher than the lumbering bomber.

Moments later Aaron noticed another Stirling, slightly below them, 250 yards (229m) away and wallowing at low speed. Then, without warning, the other

aircraft's rear gunner inexplicably began firing and raking EF452 with machine gun fire.

Within seconds the navigator lay dead at his map table, shot through the heart. Ahead of him 'Art' Aaron slumped over the controls, a wound to the head and his right arm limp and hanging on by just a few tendons. By now the Stirling was beginning a high-speed dive and Larden jumped into the right-hand seat in order to bring the bomber back onto an even keel.

Mitchem broke open the first aid kit and prepared to give the captain a shot of morphine – but before he would accept it he demanded to know what Larden's intentions were with regard to getting home. Only when he agreed to head directly back to England did Aaron accept his injection.

However, the mountainous terrain meant Larden could only route southbound and then eastwards through gaps in the granite. The crew discussed baling out over the mountain but agreed it would expose their beloved captain to further risk and injury so they pressed on towards the Italian coast. Reaching the harbour at Spezia they finally jettisoned their bombs into the sea and soon they finally managed to get a response to the emergency radio calls. They were advised not to land in Sicily (as they had planned to do) but to press on to Bone in Algeria.

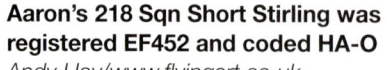

**Aaron's 218 Sqn Short Stirling was registered EF452 and coded HA-O**
*Andy Hay/www.flyingart.co.uk*

RAF armourers load sixteen 250lb bombs into a Short Stirling. The type was the largest bomber flown by the RAF during World War Two

## " Instinct kicked in and he dragged himself to the cockpit and insisted on taking over "

'Art' Aaron continued to advise the crew throughout the four-hour flight to Bone – although often only having the strength to scribble notes on pieces of paper.

Reaching the airfield the inexperienced Larden began to manoeuvre the bomber for a landing but was advised that a Vickers Wellington had crashed onto the runway. The bomb aimer therefore decided to make a belly landing next to the runway – but at that moment Aaron roused from his morphine induced slumbers yet again. Instinct kicked in and

he dragged himself to the cockpit and insisted on taking over. The two gunners lifted him into the pilot's seat and he began the let down towards the airfield. However, he could only communicate by nodding his head and was also unaware of the crashed Wellington. At the last moment he nodded an order to Larden to open the throttles and 'go-around' – and fortunately there was enough fuel to do so.

On the next approach Aaron was unhappy with the approach and ordered another attempt. The same

thing happened on the third and fourth attempts and on the fifth approach Aaron was equally unhappy but Larden refused to open the throttles as the fuel tanks were now all but empty. The aircraft ploughed into the sand alongside the main runway and quickly came to a halt. It was now 6.00am.

The emergency services extracted the crew from the aircraft and Aaron was immediately sent for surgery. However, it was too late and he succumbed to his injuries at around 3.00pm. The 21-year-old had sacrificed himself to ensure his crew got home safely and he was justifiably awarded the VC for his efforts.

# Record Breaking Medal

**When Bill Reid's VC was sold at auction in 2009 it fetched a then record breaking £348,000. However, the act of bravery that earned him the medal and saved his crew is priceless**

William 'Bill' Reid was born in Baillieston, Lanarkshire, Scotland on December 21, 1921 as the son of a blacksmith. He studied metallurgy at college and decided to apply to the RAF, qualifying as a Flight Lieutenant and joining 61 Sqn at RAF Syerston, Nottinghamshire on September 6, 1943. His first sortie over occupied Germany was on August 30 when he flew as second pilot on a 9 Sqn Lancaster on a mission to Munchen-Gladbach.

Reid would fly seven more sorties with 61 Sqn before he and his regular crew were detailed to perform an attack on Dusseldorf on the evening of November 3, 1943.

Allocated Lancaster LM360 – coded QR-O – Reid joined a flight of approximately 600 bombers given the same target. Accompanying him were Flt Sgts J A Jefferies (navigator), Les Rolton (bomb aimer), J W Norris (flight engineer), J J Mann (wireless operator), D Baldwin DFM (mid-upper gunner) and A F 'Joe' Emerson (rear gunner).

LM360 departed Syerston at 4.59pm. It was at 21,000ft (6,400m) when it reached the Netherlands but suddenly the windscreen was sprayed with cannon shells from a Messerschmitt Bf110 night fighter.

Reid felt blood trickling down his face - his body was riddled with pieces of shattered Perspex. Instinctively he pulled down his goggles to protect his eyes from the icy slipstream and although the bomber quickly lost 2,000ft (610m) he was able to regain control. However his instruments and elevator

**William Reid VC
(December 21, 1921 – November 28, 2001)**

were badly damaged and the hydraulics also took a hit.

Jeffries radioed the captain to ask how he was but Reid simply replied "I feel alright" and bravely elected to continue to Dusseldorf, despite needing hard left rudder at all times to counter the effect of the damaged elevator!

Moments later a Focke Wulf Fw 190 raked the bomber with gunfire killing the navigator instantly and seriously injuring the wireless operator. The flight engineer was also hit and Reid suffered yet more injuries. Furthermore the gun turrets were damaged and the aircraft's oxygen system disabled.

Norris clipped an oxygen bottle onto

the captain and helped to control the aircraft as it levelled out again, this time at 17,000ft (5,182m).

Still Reid continued with the mission and an hour later he overflew the target allowing Rolton to drop his bombs.

Navigating by the stars, Reid turned for home, linking his weakened arms around the control column to maintain sufficient back pressure to keep the nose from dropping.

As they coasted out over the North Sea the portable oxygen supply finally ran out; a faint-feeling Norris forgot to change over the fuel tanks and all four engines simultaneously cut. The Lancaster stalled and entered a spin but fortunately the crew were sufficiently conscious to recognise the problem, return the aircraft to level flight, switch fuel tanks and restart all four engines!

Arriving back over Britain, Reid descended to a warmer altitude, but this meant his wounds opened up again and blood began to poor down his face, obscuring his vision. Shortly before 10.00pm he spotted an airfield and eased his shot-up Lancaster onto the tarmac at the USAAF base at Shipdham, Norfolk. The damaged undercarriage collapsed and LM360 scraped to a halt. Emergency services took the crew to the base's medical bay where Mann died of his injuries the following day.

All surviving members of the crew were awarded gallantry medals – Norris received a Conspicuous Gallantry Medal (CGM), Emerson got a DFM and Reid received his Victoria Cross from King George VI at Buckingham Palace on the June 11, 1944. ❖

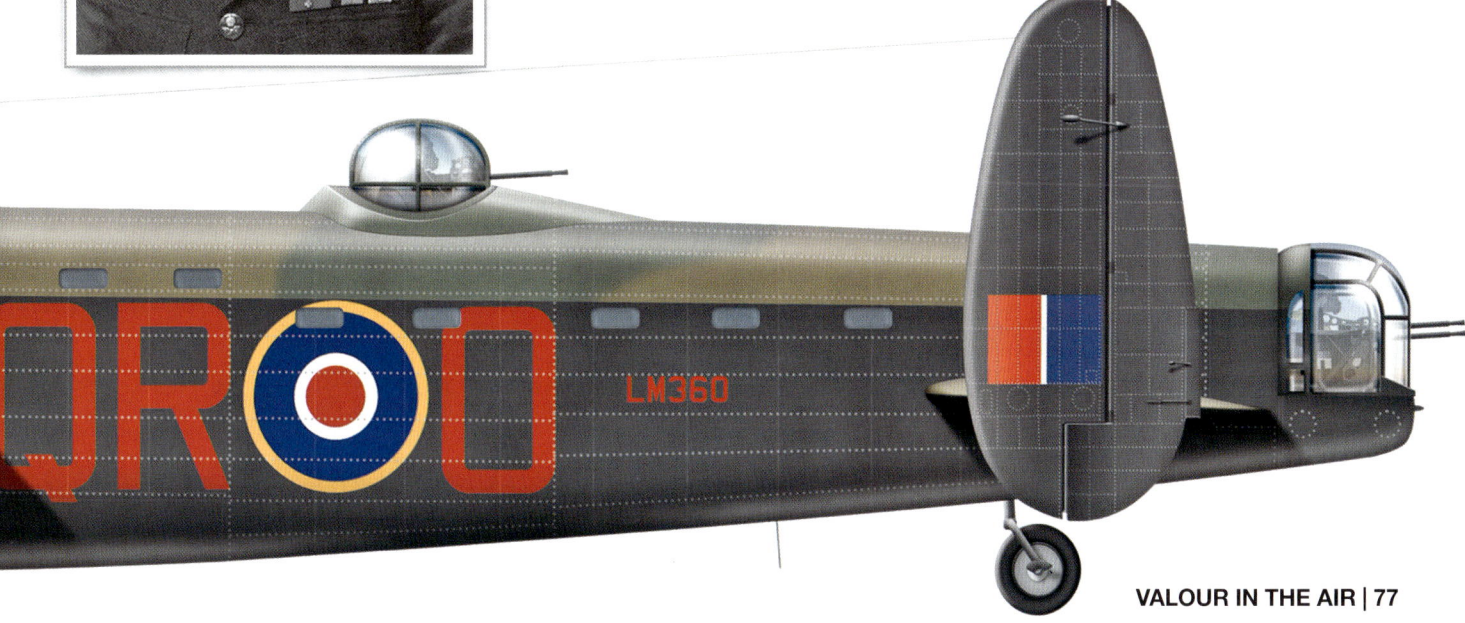

▲ LM360 was at 21,000ft over the Netherlands when suddenly the windscreen was sprayed with cannon shells from a Messerschmitt Bf110 night fighter

◄ When Reid's medal came up for auction in 2009 it was sold to an anonymous bidder for a world record £348,000. It was later revealed that it had been sold to Melissa John, who bought the medal in memory of her late brother, Christopher John, who was well known as a collector of RAF medals and whose ambition was to own a VC

Reid's Lancaster B.III was registered LM360 and wore the 61 Sqn codes QR-O *Andy Hay/www.flyingart.co.uk*

LM360

# Bomber Command's only Halifax VC

**Although Bomber Command pilots were awarded the bulk of aviation's Victoria Crosses in World War Two just one went to a Halifax pilot; this is his story.**

Cyril Joe Barton – 'Cy' to his friends and crewmates – was born in the small Suffolk village of Elveden on June 5, 1921. Aged 16 he became an apprentice engineer at the Parnall Aircraft Factory in Tolworth, Greater London and as this was a 'reserved' occupation he was exempt from being called up for military service. However, on April 16, 1941 – at the age of 19 – he put himself forward for the RAF Volunteer Reserves.

Cy travelled to the USA for basic training in late 1941 and had his first ever flight on January 17 the following year. He soloed less than a month later and after graduating as a Sergeant Pilot he returned to Britain in November 1942. Early in 1943 he joined 19 OTU at RAF Kinloss, Morayshire where he hand selected the crew he would go to war with. These men consisted of navigator Sgt J L 'Len' Lambert, bomb aimer F/O Wally Crate, wireless operator P/O Jack Kat and air gunner Sgt Freddie Brice.

The crew trained on ageing Armstrong Whitworth Whitley bombers before being posted to 1663 Heavy Conversion Unit at Rufforth, Yorkshire to learn how to operate the Handley Page Halifax. During this time two

**Cyril Joe Barton, VC**
**(June 5, 1921 – March 31, 1944)**

more members of crew joined the team: Sgt Maurice Trousdale (flight engineer) and Sgt Harry Wood (air gunner). With training complete the crew were allocated to 78 Sqn at Breighton, Yorkshire to begin their operational flying, although Barton had already performed a number of missions as second pilot with other crews by this stage.

The crew's first mission as a combined unit took place on September 15, 1943 and over the following weeks they flew regular sorties over occupied Europe. On November 11 their aircraft was hit by flak, injuring Lambert and Crate, but Barton brought it safely back to Britain and performed a safe emergency landing.

After a period of recuperation Barton's men restarted flying on November 25 and continued to do so throughout the winter; moving to 578 Sqn at RAF Snaith, Yorkshire in January and then to RAF Burn near Selby, Yorkshire the following month.

On March 30, 1944 Cy Barton and his crew strapped into Halifax LK797 – coded E for Excalibur – and prepared for a mission to Nuremberg, more than 600 miles (966km) over the German border. They would be part of a 782-strong bomber stream attacking the target that night.

Barton's Halifax lifted off at 10.12pm and climbed into a cloudless sky with a bright moon – there would be no hiding from the night fighters this evening. That said, the crew almost reached the target without being bothered by either flak or enemy aircraft 35 miles (56km) from Nuremburg the aircraft

**Cyril Barton's 578 Sqn Halifax was LK797 and carried the codes LK-E. It was known as E for Excalibur and carried nose art to that effect**
*Andy Hay/www.flyingart.co.uk*

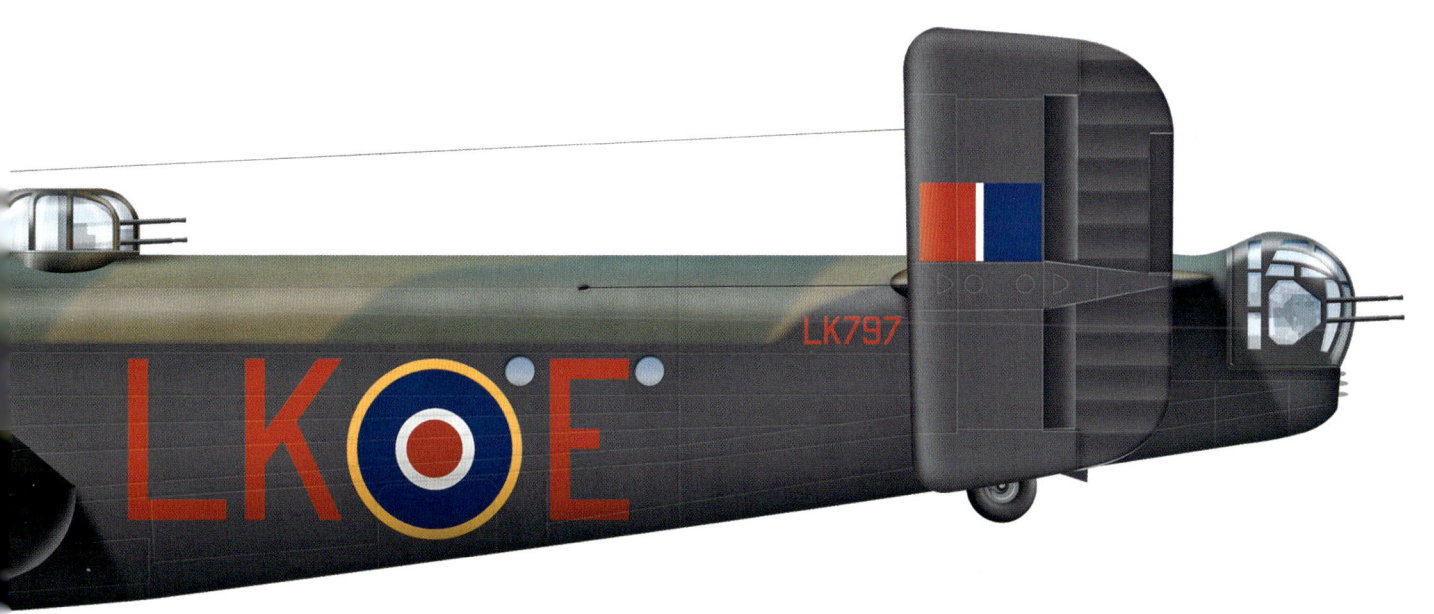

A total of 6,176 Handley Page Halifax's were built but just one 'Halibag' crew were involved in Victoria Cross winning action. This is a Halifax B.III, similar to Barton's and cleary showing the variant's later rectangular fins and Bristol Hercules radial engines

The wrecked rear fuselage of Barton's Halifax lying in Ryhope Colliery following the accident

were spotted by a Junkers Ju 88 which dropped parachute flares to illuminate them for other fighters to begin their attacks. Within minutes 50 bombers had fallen to German guns and then, as Barton began his turn towards the target, two fighters attacked head on. Seconds later the starboard inner engine was ablaze, the radios had been knocked out and the rear turret controls had been disabled. Two of the fuel tanks had also been punctured and the crew intercom lines were severed.

Quickly the Ju 88 also swung in for its attack and Barton instinctively threw the Halifax into an evasive corkscrew manoeuvre. In the tail Brice tried to fire at the Luftwaffe aircraft but his guns had been disabled. The aggressive manoeuvring forced the Germans to break off their attack and communicating by Morse code alone Barton and his crew decided to press on with their attack.

However, no sooner than Barton had levelled out the bomber the Ju 88 swung in again and more shells ripped into the bomber. Another corkscrew was initiated but this time it resulted in the disabled engine shedding its propeller amidst a shower of sparks and fire – but the German vanished yet again, albeit briefly.

On the Ju 88's next pass Harry Wood was able to loose off a salvo of tracer fire and it was seen to strike the aggressor, which then dived out of sight as Barton continued to

## "The navigator, bomb aimer and wireless operator had mistaken the Morse code for 'parachute' and baled out"

corkscrew the large bomber to a lower altitude. The German never returned.

By now the aircraft was badly damaged and had also lost a large amount of fuel from its punctured tanks. Worse still, the navigator, bomb aimer and wireless operator had mistaken the Morse code R (for 'Resume level flight') for P ('parachute') and had baled out – leaving just four people aboard the Halifax! Undeterred, Barton and his colleagues elected to press on with their attack – using only the stars for navigation. They dropped their bombs on the target and then turned for home.

The long journey back to Britain was problematic due to the lack of a navigator or serviceable navigation equipment and it is thought that LK797 cruised up the east coast of England without seeing land for many hours before finally coming ashore in County Durham. By now the fuel tanks were almost dry and the engines died just as Barton saw a row of houses in the colliery village of Ryhope. A wing struck a chimney and then the aircraft dived into a property at the end of

the row before demolishing a railway bridge. The rear section, containing Trousdale, Brice and Wood, fell into the railway cutting and the rest of the aircraft was scattered widely, killing a passing miner in the process. It was just before 6.00am and other miners returning from the night shift rescued the airmen and sent them to hospital. Sadly Cyril Barton was dead by the time he arrived. He was just 22 years old.

Barton's bravery had saved the lives of his crew and after his death a letter he had written was delivered to his mother. It read: "I hope that you will never receive this letter, but I quite expect that you will. I know what "Ops." over Germany means, and I have no illusions about it. By my own calculations the average lifespan of an aircrew is 20 operations." The attack on Nuremberg was Barton's 19th sortie.

For his actions in the attack on Nuremberg Barton was awarded the Victoria Cross posthumously in June 1944. Today, a housing estate in Ryhope is named Barton Park in his honour and a nearby street is named Halifax Place. ❖

# Victory IN EUROPE

## 75TH ANNIVERSARY SPECIAL

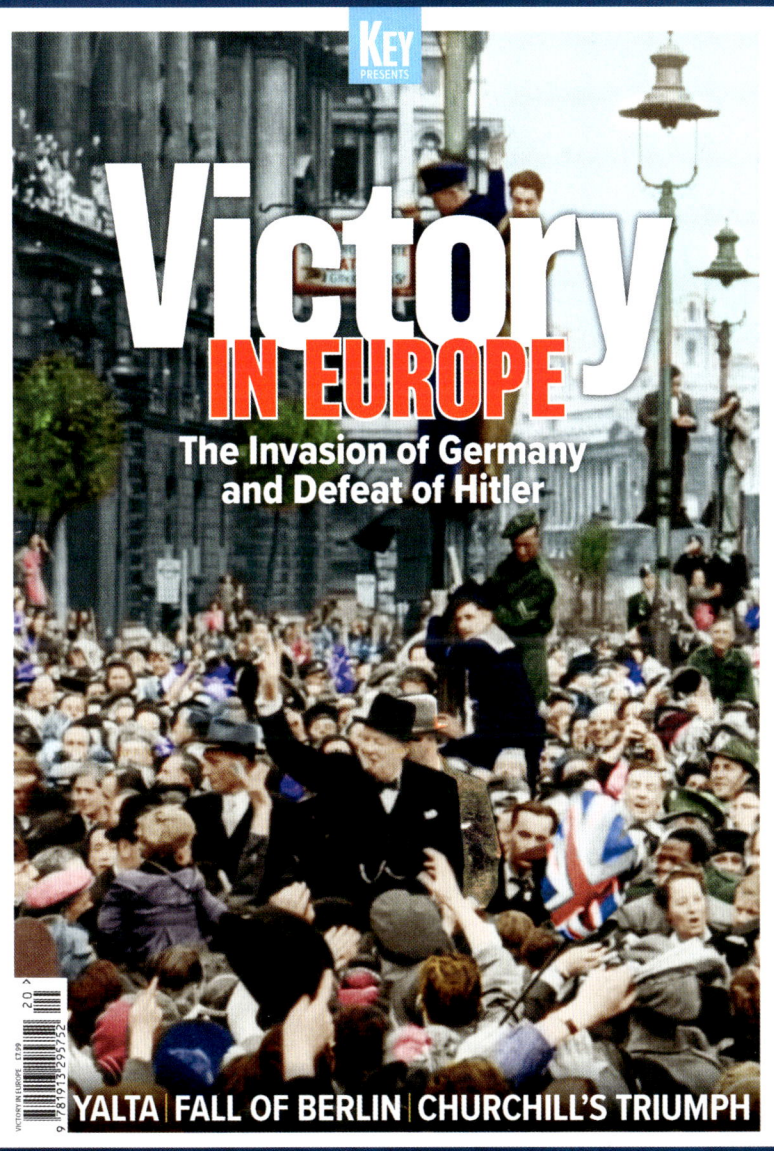

As early as January 1943, when Hitler's 6th Army was destroyed at Stalingrad, it was evident that the war in Europe could only end with the defeat of the Third Reich.

Yet the Germans fought on, as the Soviet forces inflicted one crushing defeat after another on the Eastern Front.

What drove the German people to fight on, knowing that ruin and devastation was the inevitable consequence? Why did the generals continue to follow Hitler's orders? Did the Allies win the war in Europe, or did Hitler lose it?

All this and more is covered in this 100-page special publication detailing the invasion of Germany and the defeat of Hitler.

# Award Winning Flight Engineer

## Although the majority of aviation-related VCs were awarded to pilots, one did go to a Flight Engineer – this is Norman Jackson's story

Norman Cyril Jackson was born in Ealing, Middlesex on April 8, 1919 and was adopted by the Gunter family while he was a small baby.

After schooling he qualified as an engineering fitter and turner; a career that meant he was exempt from enlistment. Nevertheless, he decided to volunteer for military service and joined the RAF Volunteer Reserve in 1939. Jackson initially served as an engine fitter and in January 1941 he was assigned to a 95 Sqn, which was operating Sunderland flying boats on the West African coast near Freetown, Sierra Leone.

He continued in this role for 18 months but the opportunity to retrain for flying duties tempted him and he applied for training to become a flight engineer; returning to Britain in September 1942 to begin his studies.

By mid-1943 he had been promoted to Sergeant and on July 28 he joined 106 Sqn at RAF Syerston, Nottinghamshire to become a flight engineer on Avro Lancasters.

Sgt Jackson was assigned to F/O Fred Mifflin's crew and by April 1944 he had completed 30 operational sorties and was deemed to have completed his 'tour', However, by virtue of standing in for another flight engineer that had 'gone sick', Jackson had accumulated one more mission than his squadron mates –but he volunteered to fly one extra trip to Germany "just for luck" to bomb the Schweinfurt ball bearing factories, some 50 miles (80km)

**Norman Cyril Jackson VC (April 8, 1919 – March 26, 1994)**

northwest of Nuremberg.

On April 26 the crew strapping into Lancaster ME669 – coded ZN-O – were in good spirits, especially Jackson, whose wife, Alma, had just given birth to their first son. The Lancaster launched from Syerston at 9.32pm, battling against an un-forecast headwind. By the time Miffin reached the target they were some way behind the other bombers but had met no opposition.

However, as the crew began the run for home a 'blip' on the Lancaster's radar screen revealed an inbound night fighter and Mifflin began to corkscrew the bomber in an attempt to evade the enemy. But he was too slow and

cannon fire raked the bomber as a Focke Wulf FW 190 made a hit and run attack, causing the Lancaster's starboard inner engine to burst into flames. Jackson pushed the fire extinguisher button and saw the flames die away briefly before re-igniting at an even more ferocious rate.

He immediately strapped on his parachute, grabbed a fire extinguisher and opened the escape hatch. "I'll climb out onto the wing" he told the pilot "that'll fix it."

Jackson opened his parachute inside the cabin and instructed other crewmembers to hold onto the canopy as he edged out onto the wing. Seeing a handhold on the wing he threw himself out against the 175kts (200mph) slipstream until he could hold onto the engine intake and then pointed the fire extinguisher nozzle into the flames. Gripping the aeroplane with just one hand he kept the flow of extinguishing gas pointing inside the engine cowling and was gratified to see the flames finally die back.

He was just beginning to make his way back towards the cabin when the German fighter returned and fired on him. Feeling intense pain in his legs and back, Jackson involuntarily released his grip on the aircraft. The airflow whipped him backwards off the wing and past the now-burning tailplane before his parachute lines became taut. It was then that he noticed the fire had almost burned through the lines and they were smouldering.

Back inside the Lancaster Mifflin

**The Lancaster in which Norman Jackson was flying on the mission for which he was awarded the VC was registered ME669 and wore the 106 Sqn codes WN-O**
*Andy Hay/www.flyingart.co.uk*

Jackson initially served with 95 Sqn as an engine fitter on Short Sunderland flying boats off the West African coast near Sierra Leone

Lancasters would drop more than 600,000 tonnes of bombs during around 156,000 operational sorties across World War Two ▶ In late 1942 Jackson returned to the UK to retrain as a wireless operator on Avro Lancasters. Here an example is bombed up prior to a mission over Occupied Europe

gave the order to bale out and the crewmembers holding onto Jackson's parachute canopy released it. Jackson used his hands to extinguish his smouldering parachute lines but there was little he could do to stop the holes burnt into the silk canopy from splitting. He descended at a rapid rate, although the parachute did slow his fall sufficiently to mean he was still alive when he landed heavily in a bush; breaking both ankles in the process. He also had leg and back injuries from his 'run-in' with the Fw 190 and had severe burns on his hands.

Fred Mifflin and Hugh Johnson (the tailgunner) had been unable to bale out and were killed when the Lancaster crashed. The other survivors were quickly picked up by German patrols and spent the rest of the war in various prison camps.

Despite his injuries Jackson survived the night and began to look for help. Crawling on his knees and elbows he made his way to a house where he was met by an angry German. Minutes later the police arrived and – despite his injuries – Jackson was made to walk to the nearest town where locals jeered

and threw stones at him.

For the next ten months Norman Jackson remained in a German hospital before he was moved to a prison camp. On his second escape attempt he managed to meet the Americans near Munich.

When the other survivors were repatriated to England at the end of the war Jackson's bravery became apparent and he was immediately recommended for the Victoria Cross. The citation of his award was announced in the *London Gazette* on October 26, 1945, describing Jackson's actions as "most incredible." ❖

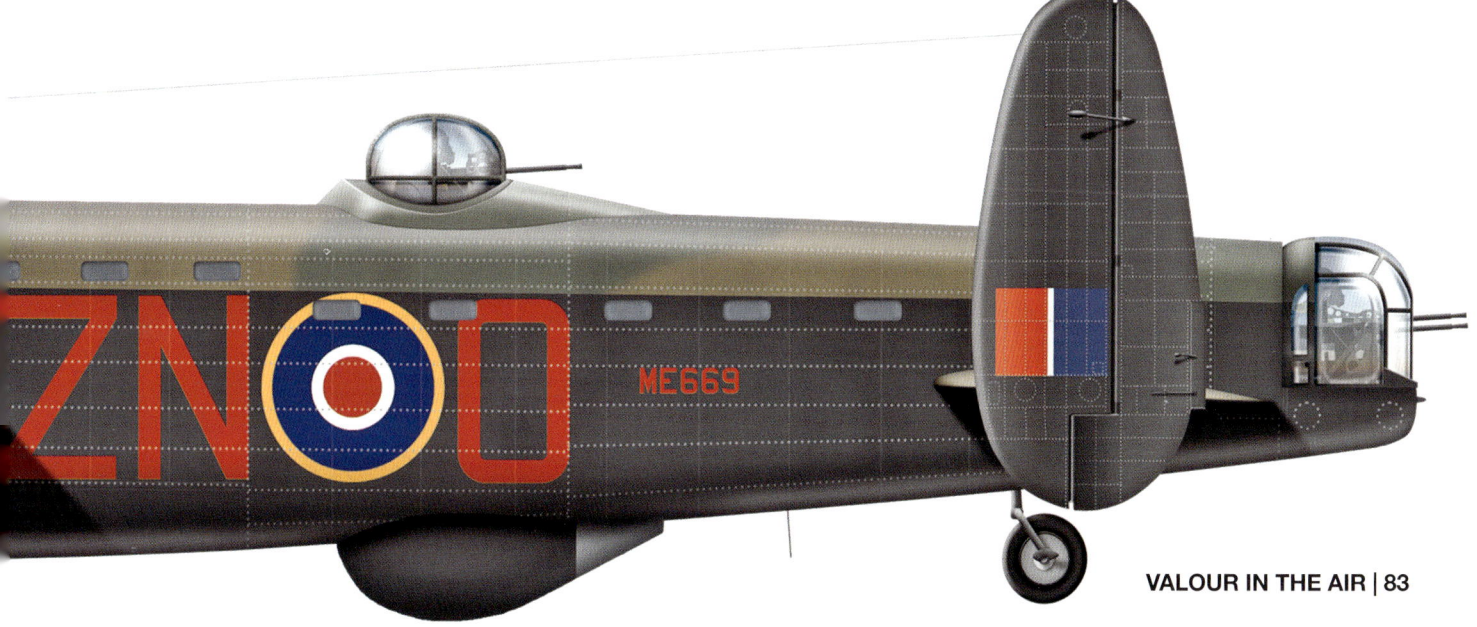

# Selfless Bravery to Save a Trapped Colleague

## Canadian born Andrew Mynarski was the first of three Canadian airmen to receive the VC for feats of aerial valour during World War Two

The son of Polish/Canadian parents Andrew Charles Mynarski was born in Winnipeg, Manitoba on October 14, 1916. His father passed away when he was just 16 years old and to help support his mother and five siblings he began work as a chamois cutter and furrier.

However, at the onset of World War Two Mynarski enrolled in the military, initially serving with the Royal Winnipeg Rifles in 1940 before enlisting in the Royal Canadian Air Force (RCAF) on September 29, 1941.

Following initial recruit training he began to learn the skills involved in becoming a Wireless Air Gunner (WAG) at No 2 Wireless School in Calgary in March 1942 before transferring to No 3 Bombing and Gunnery School in Manitoba.

Upon qualification he was promoted to Sergeant and sailed to Britain from New York Harbor on January 5, 1943.

Upon reaching England, Mynarski joined 16 OTU for further training before being allocated to 1661 Heavy Conversion Unit. He then moved to 9 Sqn at RAF Bardney, Lincolnshire for further training on October 31 and was promoted to Flight Sergeant. By December 18 he had become a Warrant Officer II and on April 10, 1944 he joined the RCAF's 419 'Moose' Sqn at RAF

**Andrew Charles Mynarski VC
(October 14, 1916 – June 13, 1944)**

Middleton St George in County Durham (today Durham Tees Valley Airport).

The unit was the third RCAF bomber squadron to be formed, and by the time Mynarski joined it was equipped with the Handley Page Halifax. His first operational sortie finally came on the night of April 22/23 in Halifax III HR925 but just five days later the squadron swapped its 'Halibags' for Avro Lancaster Xs.

Mynarsaki's first Lancaster sortie

occurred on May 1 and the crew he was allocated to quickly began to 'gel'. The team was led by pilot F/O Arthur 'Art' de Breyne alongside navigator F/O Robert Body, air bomber Sgt Jack Friday, wireless operator W/O Jimmy Kelly and air gunners F/O George Brophy and Andrew Mynarski himself. The flight engineer, Sgt Roy Vigars, was the only Englishman among the all-Canadian crew and in late June 1944 they were allocated their 'own' Lancaster – KB726, coded VR-A.

On the evening of June 12, 1944 – operating in the aftermath of the D-Day landings – the crew of VR-A were tasked with its 13th operational mission. Unbeknown to Mynarski his commission as a pilot officer had been approved the previous day.

The aircraft took off from Middleton St George at 9.44pm carrying sixteen 500lb (227kg) 'general purpose' (GP) bombs and a pair of 500lb (227kg) long-delay bombs en route to the marshalling yards at Cambrai in northern France. It was a clear, cloudless night and this was to be a rare low-level mission, dropping the bombs from just 2,000ft (610m).

Approaching the target intensive flak batteries opened up against the bombers but VR-A managed to evade the shells. The crew were not so lucky when a lone Junker Ju-88 night fighter

▲ Part of Canada's contribution to World War Two was 15 heavy bomber squadrons known as RCAF 6 Group

◄ Perhaps the most famous warbird flying in the colours of a VC holder is the Canadian Warplane Heritage Museum's Lancaster X. The aircraft has worn Mynarski's markings since it returned to flight in 1988
*KEY – Duncan Cubitt*

▼ Mynarski's Lancaster was registered KB726 and wore the VR-A codes of the RCAF's 419 'Moose' Sqn
*Andy Hay/www.flyingart.co.uk*

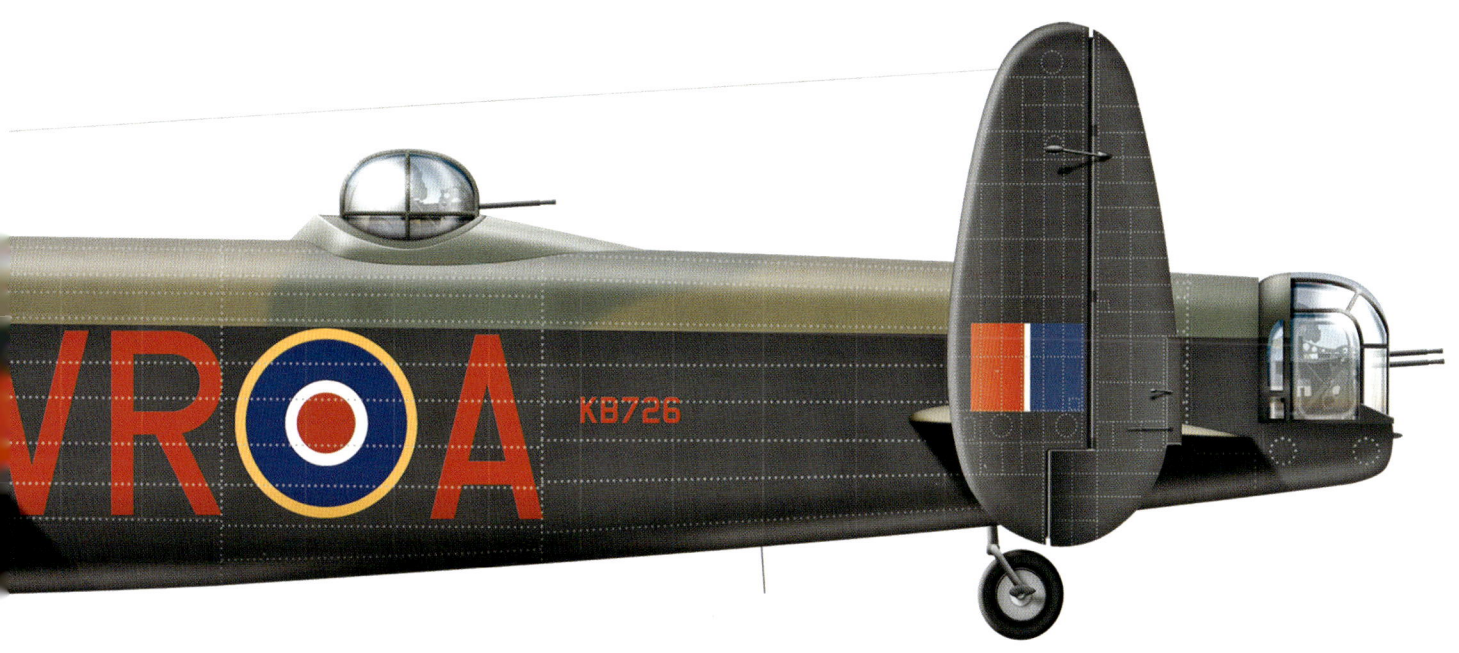

Of the 120,000 who served in Bomber Command, 55,573 were killed including over 10,000 Canadians

appeared on their port side and began firing its cannons. The bomber took several direct hits and immediately both port engines stopped; their propellers windmilling to a swift halt just as an intense fire broke out in the rear fuselage behind Mynarski's upper turret.

Further aft, George Brophy's rear turret had borne the brunt of the attack and its hydraulic lines were damaged beyond repair. This left him with just a winding handle to manually operate the turret and affect his escape – but within a few turns the handle snapped. When the captain gave the order to bail out Brophy was trapped and unable to exit the burning aeroplane unaided.

Five crewmembers ultimately left the stricken Lancaster through the front escape hatch on the floor of the cockpit, but not without incident. When bomb aimer Jack Friday tried to release the escape hatch cover the rushing wind ripped it from his hands. The hatch hit him above his left eye and knocked him out causing him to fall onto hatch and jamming it closed. It was the flight engineer, Roy Vigars, who clipped a parachute onto Friday's unconscious body and tossed him out the hatch while simultaneously pulling the ripcord.

The other airmen followed but it was at this point that Andrew Mynarski put all thoughts of his own escape aside and made his way towards the fire in an attempt to release his friend and colleague. Within seconds his lower half was drenched in burning hydraulic fuel

**Mynarski and his crewmates departed from RAF Middleton St George for their final mission. Today the airfield is called Durham Tees Valley Airport and this statue of a saluting Mynarski greets visitors.**

yet still he made his way through the flames towards the tail gunner.

All his efforts to open the turret were in vain, initially using a fire axe to try to pry open the doors before finally resorting to beating at the turret with his hands. Finally, with Mynarski's flight

suit and parachute on fire and knowing how close to the ground the aircraft was Brophy yelled at his mate to give up and leave him before it was too late. Reluctantly, Mynarski made his way back to the escape hatch but before he jumped he turned back to Brophy, straightened up and saluted farewell. He then plunged through the hatch, with his clothes and parachute alight.

Amazingly the plucky Canadian survived the fall but died shortly afterwards from his horrific burns.

Even more amazingly, as the blazing VR-A hit the ground Brophy was thrown clear of his turret and survived – as did the other members of the crew, all of whom were captured by the Germans and spent the remainder of the war in POW camps.

Andrew Mynarski's deliberate delaying of his own escape in an attempt to rescue his comrade was not forgotten and when the crew of KB726 were repatriated at the end of the war he was awarded a posthumous Victoria Cross on October 11, 1946. The citation summed up his valour by saying "P/O Mynarski must have been fully aware that in trying to free the rear gunner he was almost certain to lose his own life. Despite this, with outstanding courage and complete disregard for his own safety, he went to the rescue. Willingly accepting the danger, P/O Mynarski lost his life by a most conspicuous act of heroism which called for valour of the highest order." ❖

# After Ordeal by Fire Comes Ordeal by Water

## David Hornell was flying a Coastal Command mission in a Canadian Consolidated Canso, but lost his life in a dinghy in the middle of the ocean

David Ernest Hornell was born on Toronto Island, Canada on January 26, 1910 and during his school years he proved to be both academically gifted and an accomplished sportsman.

Despite winning a scholarship he opted not to pursue a university education and joined the Goodyear Tire & Rubber Company to work in the research laboratories. He was carving a successful career by the time war broke out but he was unable to avoid the urge to enlist and on January 8, 1941 he joined the Royal Canadian Air Force (RCAF). Three weeks later he turned 31; the age at which he would have been exempt from uniformed service.

Hornell undertook his basic training at various locations in mainland Canada and received his 'wings' as a commissioned Pilot Officer on September 25, 1941.

The following month he joined 120 Sqn RCAF at Coal Harbour, Nova Scotia where he began flying operational missions in ageing Supermarine Stranraer biplane seaplanes protecting Canada's eastern seaboard. He

**David Ernest Hornell VC**
**(January 26, 1910 –June 24, 1944)**

remained in this role for two years (although he never saw a single U-Boat) and was promoted to Flying Officer and then Flight Lieutenant before being sent to the USA in 1943 to act as a test pilot at Boeing. There he assessed various

aircraft being built for the RCAF before he finally got his wish to be deployed to a frontline unit.

In December 1943 he was allocated to 162 Sqn RCAF and began training on the Consolidated Canso (as the Catalina was known in RCAF service). On the last day of the year he was sent to Reykjavik, Iceland and on January 25, 1944 he performed his first operational patrol.

Although the Canso was a significant improvement over the Stranraer it was still slow and under-armed for the anti-submarine role but on May 24 Hornell and his crew were despatched to Wick, Scotland on a 162 Sqn detachment to patrol the North Sea.

On June 24 Hornell was to make his 61st and final operational sortie. Flying Canso 9754 – coded P – he was commanding a crew a seven Canadians; consisting of navigator F/O S E 'Ed' Matheson, second pilot F/O Bernard Denomy, flight engineers Sgt D S Scott and Sgt Bernard St Laurant and air gunners F/O Graham Campbell, Flt Sgt Israel 'Joe' Bodnoff and Flt Sgt Sydney Cole.

**Hornell's Consolidated Canso at rest in early 1944**
*RCAF Archives*

The Canso eased into the skies from Wick at 9.30am and the crew spent the remainder of the day searching in vain for German vessels. Finally, at 7.00pm, Hornell turned for home. They were north of the Shetland Islands and had been flying for almost ten hours when Bodnoff and Cole in the port observation blister spotted a submarine. It was fully surfaced and just 5 miles (8km) away.

Unbeknown to the crew this was the German Navy's new 251ft 10in (76.76m)-long U-1225, which had departed Kristiansand on her first mission just four days earlier with 56 sailors aboard.

Hornell immediately swung the flying boat into an attack profile and descended towards the U-Boat. However, 4 miles (6.5km) from the target the German crew began to open fire with their flak guns.

The first hit took out the Canso's radio aerials and during the two minutes it took to reach the submarine the aircraft was hit numerous times. The tailplane was severely damaged but Hornell maintained the straight and level track needed to successfully release the depth charges.

Next, a direct hit on the port engines caused it to catch alight; the flames soon spreading to the trailing edge of the wing. At 1,200 yards (1,097m) the Canso's manually operated .303in Browning machine guns in the nose and the blisters came into operational range and the crew could finally begin firing back at the enemy.

Passing 800 yards (731m) U-1225's guns fell quiet as the ship's commander ordered the submarine to turn in an attempt to present as small a target as possible to the inbound bomber.

Moments later Hornell and his crew roared over the vessel at just 50ft (15.2m) and dropped the entire load of depth charges in a perfect straddle. Moments later, the U-Boat's bow reared upwards and landed back into the water with a huge plume of spray. It would sink within minutes without a single survivor.

Back in the air Hornell managed to coax the damaged Canso up to an altitude of 250ft (76m) before the burning engine fell from its molten mounts. The resulting leaks of fuel and oil ignited further fires in the wing and it was obvious that the aircraft would need to ditch if the crew stood any chance of survival. Hornell turned the bomber into wind and, skimming the 12ft (3.6m) waves, gently put it down onto the ocean. It immediately bounced back into the skies, reaching 150ft (45.7m) before it settled back onto the ocean, still ablaze.

Just 5 minutes later the entire crew had evacuated into the life rafts, having first grabbed the emergency ration boxes and water. Less than 10 minutes later Canso 9754 sank, following U-1225 to the ocean floor.

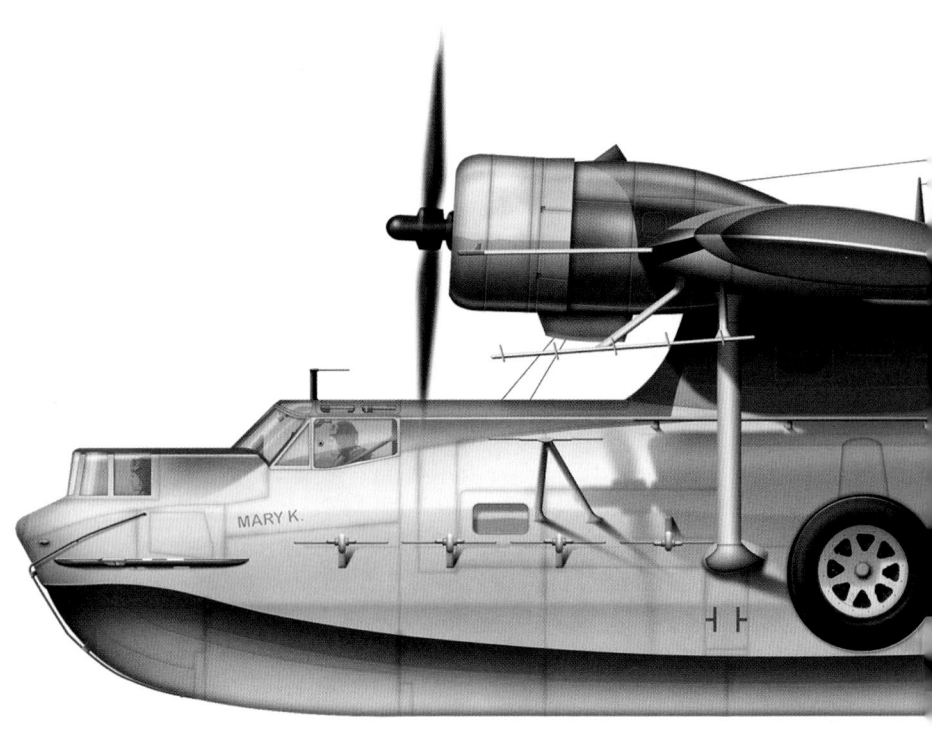

Seven of the crew were crammed into a single four-man life raft and soon they noticed St Laurant, about 100ft (30.5m) away, who was wrestling to right the second dinghy, which had overturned as he'd thrown it clear of the aircraft.

Campbell and Matheson dived into the water and went to his assistance and briefly righted the dinghy before it was caught in a strong gust of wind. This ejected the three men into the water and blew the raft out of range. The eight crewmembers now had to cram into a single dinghy and they took it in turns with four sitting in the raft and four clinging onto the outside, submerged up to their necks in the freezing North Sea water.

Using a pair of trousers with knotted ankles to bail out the dinghy gave some more room and as night fell all eight men managed to cram inside the boat – apart from Scott, whose legs still dangled into the sea.

During the night the sea swell picked up and 50kt (57mph) winds resulted in 40ft (12.2m) waves. Nonetheless they managed to stay in the dinghy and just before midnight an RAF Catalina from 333 Sqn was spotted and Campbell fired three red distress flares.

The Norwegian pilot of the Catalina (Lt Johannsen) quickly saw the survivors and dropped sea markers before radioing back to base to request air-sea-rescue (ASR) services. Orbiting the area the Catalina used an Aldis lamp to message (in Morse Code) 'Courage – HSL [High Speed Launch] on way – help coming.'

The Catalina continued to orbit for 14 hours, by which time the dinghy had capsized several times and St Laurant had eventually succumbed to exposure and died. The crew were exhausted but two hours later they saw an ASR Vickers Warwick approaching the area. It dropped a lifeboat under a parachute but it landed 500ft (152m) away and the men were too weak to make their way towards it.

Hornell's health was worsening now and he was almost blind as a result of exposure. Undeterred he decided to swim for the newly delivered lifeboat, only for his crewmates to restrain him for his own safety. Another three hours passed at Scott became the second crewmember to succumb to the elements but still Hornell hung on offering advice and guidance to his team.

It would be yet another two hours before a Short Sunderland appeared overhead, guiding an ASR launch to the survivors. Some 20hrs and 35 minutes after they had crashed the survivors were finally pulled from the water. David Hornell passed away 20 minutes later.

For his outstanding courage in pressing home the successful attack on the submarine followed by the hours keeping alive the spirits of his crew David Hornell was posthumously awarded the Victoria Cross on July 28, 1944.

For their roles in the mission Denomy received a DSO, Campbell and Matheson each received a DFC and Cole and Bodnoff were awarded the DFM. Rules of the time meant the two dead crewmembers (Scott & St Laurent) could only be 'Mentioned in Despatches.'

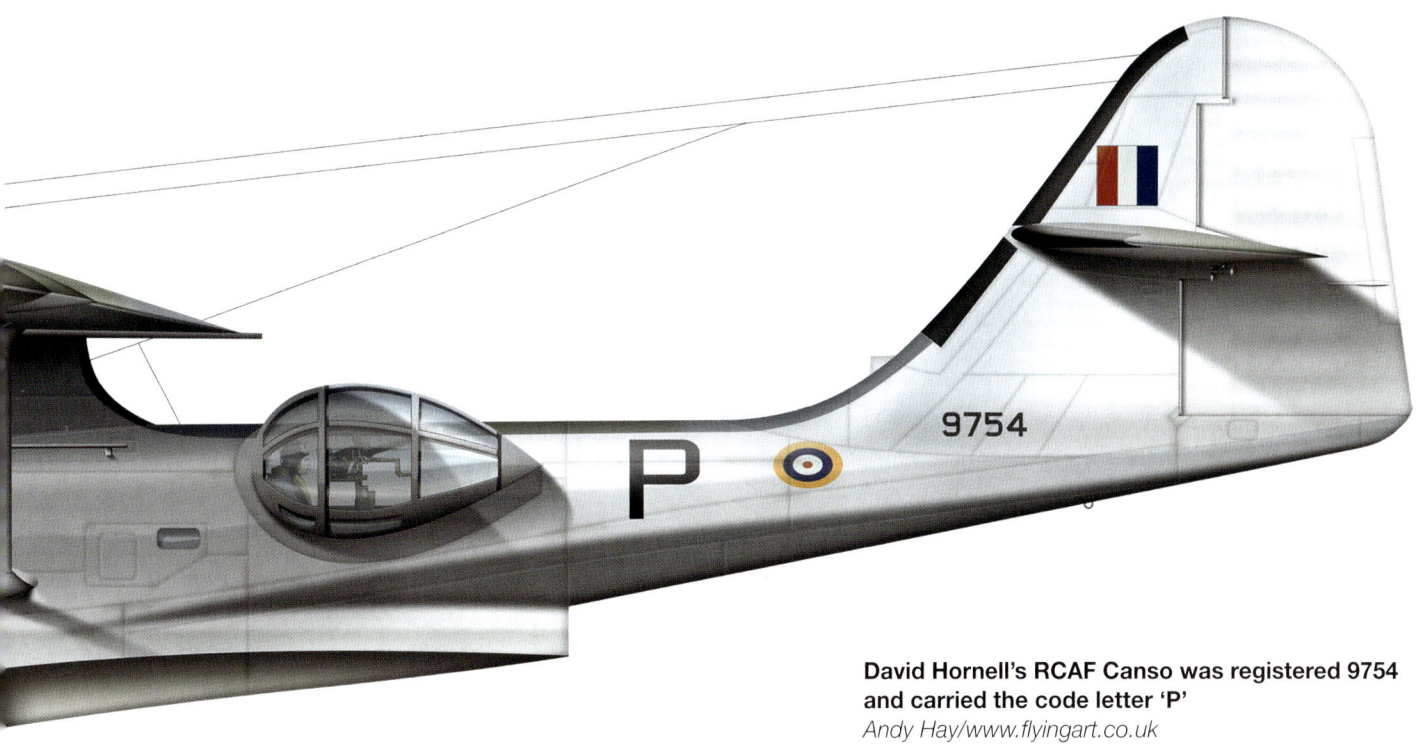

David Hornell's RCAF Canso was registered 9754 and carried the code letter 'P'
*Andy Hay/www.flyingart.co.uk*

## CITATION

The announcement and accompanying citation for the decoration was published in a supplement to the *London Gazette* on July 24, 1944. It read:

"The KING has been graciously pleased to confer the VICTORIA CROSS on the under-mentioned officer in recognition of most conspicuous bravery:

"Flt Lt David Ernest Hornell (deceased) RCAF 162 Sqn

"Flt Lt Hornell was captain and first pilot of a twin-engined amphibian aircraft engaged on an anti-submarine patrol in northern waters. The patrol had lasted for some hours when a fully-surfaced U-boat was sighted, travelling at high speed on the port beam. Flt Lt Hornell at once turned to the attack.

The U-boat altered course. The aircraft had been seen and there could be no surprise. The U-boat opened up with anti-aircraft fire which became increasingly fierce and accurate.

"At a range of 1,200 yards, the front guns of the aircraft replied; then its starboard guns jammed, leaving only one gun effective. Hits were obtained on and around the conning-tower of the U-boat, but the aircraft was itself hit, two large holes appearing in the starboard wing.

"Ignoring the enemy's fire, Flt Lt Hornell carefully manoeuvred for the attack. Oil was pouring from his starboard engine, which was, by this time, on fire, as was the starboard wing; and the petrol tanks were endangered. Meanwhile, the aircraft was hit again and again by the U-boat's guns. Holed in many places, it was vibrating violently and very difficult to control.

"Nevertheless, the captain decided to press home his attack, knowing that with every moment the chances of escape for him and his gallant crew would grow more slender. He brought his aircraft down very low and released his depth charges in a perfect straddle. The bows of the U-boat were lifted out of the water; it sank and the crew were seen in the sea.

"Flt Lt Hornell contrived, by superhuman efforts at the controls, to gain a little height. The fire in the starboard wing had grown more intense and the vibration had increased. Then the burning engine fell off. The plight of aircraft and crew was now desperate. With the utmost coolness, the captain took his aircraft into wind and, despite the manifold dangers, brought it safely down on the heavy swell. Badly damaged and blazing furiously, the aircraft rapidly settled.

After ordeal by fire came ordeal by water. There was only one serviceable dinghy and this could not hold all the crew. So they took turns in the water, holding on to the sides. Once, the dinghy capsized in the rough seas and was righted only with great difficulty. Two of the crew succumbed from exposure.

"An airborne lifeboat was dropped to them but fell some 500 yards down wind. The men struggled vainly to reach it and Flt Lt Hornell, who throughout had encouraged them by his cheerfulness and inspiring leadership, proposed to swim to it, through he was nearly exhausted. He was with difficulty restrained. The survivors were finally rescued after they had been in the water for 21 hours. By this time Flt Lt Hornell was blinded and completely exhausted. He died shortly after being picked up.

Flt Lt Hornell had completed 60 operational missions, involving 600 hours' flying. He well knew the danger and difficulties attending attacks on submarines. By pressing home a skilful and successful attack against fierce opposition, with his aircraft in a precarious condition, and by fortifying and encouraging his comrades in the subsequent ordeal, this officer displayed valour and devotion to duty of the highest order.

# The Last Survivor

## At the time of writing former RAF Coastal Command pilot John Cruickshank is 100 years old and the last living recipient to have been awarded the VC during World War Two.

John Alexander 'Jock' Cruickshank was born in Aberdeen, Scotland on May 20, 1920 and was educated at the local Grammar School before joining the Commercial Bank of Scotland as an apprentice in 1938.

With conflict seemingly imminent Cruickshank decided to volunteer for the Territorial Army a few days prior to his 19th birthday and when war was declared he was 'called up' for service in the Royal Artillery. He continued with the unit until early 1941 when he applied for a transfer to the RAF for pilot training.

Basic training began in July of that year and on September 15 he was sent to Canada for elementary flight training. On December 10, 1941 – just three days after the attack on Pearl Harbor – Cruickshank was posted to NAS Pensacola, Florida for advanced pilot instruction. By July 1942 he was finally qualified and awarded his 'wings' and commissioned as a Pilot Officer within the RAF Volunteer Reserves (RAFVR).

On his return to Britain John Cruickshank was posted to 4 (Coastal) OTU at Invergordon, Scotland for operational training on the Consolidated PBY Catalina and on

**John Alexander Cruickshank VC (Born May 20, 1920)**

January 10, 1943 he was promoted to Flying Officer.

Cruickshank was posted to his first operational unit, 120 Sqn, on March 25 and immediately began flying anti-submarine missions from its base at Sullom Voe in the Shetland Islands.

By the summer of 1944 Cruickshank had completed more than 40 operational sorties as part of Coastal

Command's battle to keep the North Atlantic and Arctic sea lanes open for supply convoys – although, in common with most of his compatriots, he had seen little in the way of action.

On July 17 'Jock' Cruickshank prepared Catalina JV928 – coded DA-Y – for what would be his 48th mission. Joining him in the 'Cat' that day would be Flt Sgt Jack Garnett (second pilot), F/O J C Dickson (navigator) Flt Sgt S B Harbison (flight engineer); two wireless operators: W/O W C Jenkins and Flt Sgt H Gershenson; and two gunners (Sgts J Appleton and R S C Proctor). Also aboard was a qualified riggor (Flt Sgt A I Cregan) and Sgt S I Fidler, the 'third pilot' looking to gain experience.

Taking off at 1.45pm and the crew began a 14-hour patrol hunting German U-boats. They failed to see a single vessel until 8.45pm when the on-board radar picked up a contact 43 miles (69km) away.

From a height of 2,000ft (610ft) Cruickshank soon saw a submarine cruising on the surface. It made no attempt to hide so he ordered his crew to fire an identification flare. In return the Catalina received a barrage of flak. They had located a Type VIIC U-boat; *U-361.* The ship had launched on

**The RAF operated both the PBY-5 seaplane and PBY-5A amphibian versions of the Consolidated Catalina**

In the 1980s and 90s privately owned PBY-5A Catalina G-BLSC operated from Duxford, Cambridgeshire in the markings of Cruickshank's JV928 *Steve Bridgewater*

An RAF Catalina returns from an anti-submarine mission

G-BLSC, operated by Plane Sailing Displays, flying in the colours of Cruickshank's Catalina. Note the lack of waist blisters or nose turret on this civilianised airframe. The 'Super Catalina' also boasted more powerful engines, a larger tail and even an air-stair to help gain access to the rear fuselage!
*KEY - Duncan Cubitt*

September 9, 1942 and had already carried out three patrols and been a member of six wolfpacks – although she had not sunk, or even damaged, any Allied ships.

Immediately Cruickshank pulled the big, lumbering patrol bomber into an attack profile and descended to 50ft (15m). Passing a range of 1,000 yards (915m) the nose turret and blister gunners began firing their .303in guns. As the Catalina roared over the vessel Cruickshank ordered depth charges to be released – but the weapons failed to drop.

The U-boat had all but stopped but flak reappeared as soon as Cruickshank resumed his attack. Seconds later the Germans scored a direct hit and a shell exploded within the bomber's fuselage. Dickson was

killed instantly; Harbison was wounded in both legs and Appleton suffered head injuries. Cruickshank received wounds to his legs and his chest but continued with the bombing run.

Reaching 50ft (15m) he tried again to loose the weapons, and this time all six depth charges released in a perfect straddle across the *U-361*. Pulling up into sea fog the crew never saw the submarine again – it was later revealed to have sunk rapidly.

Cruickshank's new priority was to get the stricken JV928 back to base. Analysis showed the hull to be riddled with shrapnel holes and flak had ripped a 1ft (30cm) gash along the waterline. The radar was also unserviceable and the fuel tanks were leaking at an alarming rate. The latter was of particular concern as Sullom Voe was

still several hundreds of miles away.

The crew got to work plugging holes with rags, canvas engine covers and even their 'Mae West' life jackets while, up front, Garnett took over flying to allow Cruickshank to have his wounds tended. It was during this treatment that the 'skipper' passed out.

It was some time before he came round, but he immediately tried to make his way back to the flight deck – only Appleton restraining him prevented him from aggravating his injuries through excessive exertion. Despite his condition Cruickshank refused morphine in fear that it would prevent him from thinking straight and he faded in and out of consciousness throughout the flight back to base.

Five and half hours later the Catalina arrived overhead Sullom Voe and

Cruickshank insisted in resuming command of the aircraft. Despite immense pain and difficulty breathing, he ordered that they orbit until first light for the best chance of a safe landing.

Catalina JV928 circled the Shetlands for the next hour as its crew jettisoned guns, armour and anything else they could to reduce the weight of the damaged airframe in readiness for landing.

As the sun was rising, Garnett and Cruickshank eased the flying boat down – at which point it immediately began to fill with water through the myriad holes in the hull. The flight crew gunned the throttles and 'flew' the Catalina straight up onto the sand at high speed, beaching it close to the waiting medical teams.

Cruickshank needed an immediate blood transfusion before being taken to the base hospital – where he was found to have 72 individual wounds.

For his bravery 'Jock' Cruickshank was awarded the VC on September 1, 1944 and Jack Garnett was presented with the DFM at a joint investiture at Holyrood House, Edinburgh.

Cruickshank's award was one of just four VCs awarded to Coastal Command crew during the war; the others were posthumous. 'Jock' never returned to operational flying and eventually left the RAF in 1946 to continue his career in banking and international finance. Today, at the age of 100, he remains a vice chairman of The Victoria Cross and George Cross Association along with Gurkha, Rambahadur Limbu. ❖

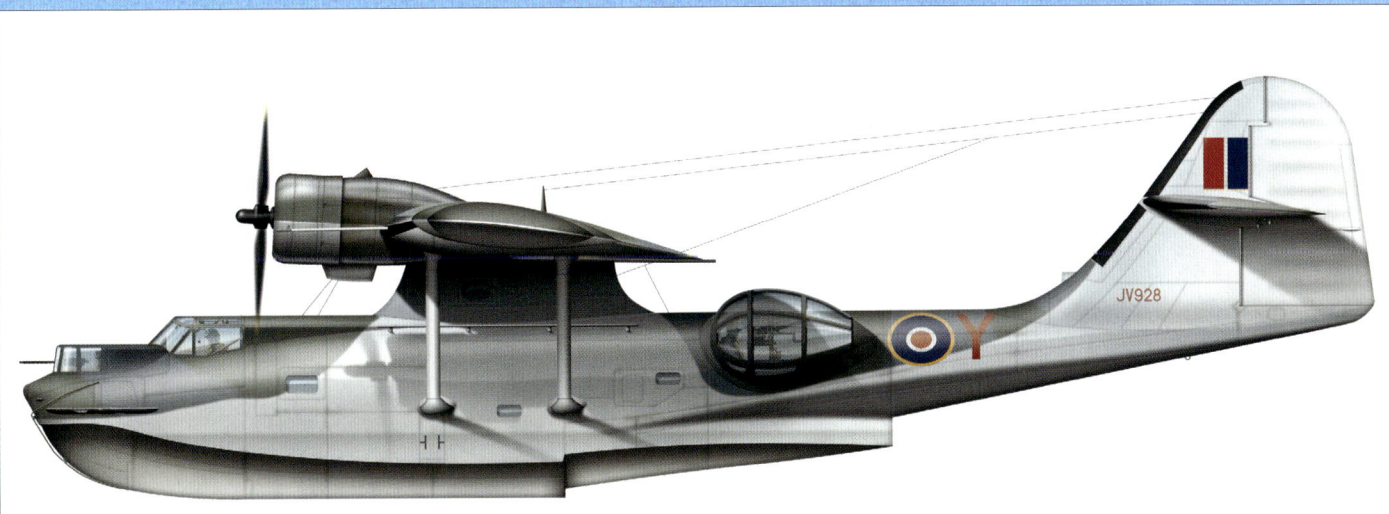

**John Cruickshank's 120 Sqn PBY Catalina was registered JV928 and coded DA-Y** *Andy Hay/www.flyingart.co.uk*

# The First Pathfinder VC

**Although a bomber crew's 'tour' was 30 operational sorties, many volunteered to fly additional missions; one such pilot was Ian Bazalgette, who was lost on his 54th trip**

Ian Willoughby Bazalgette was born to English parents living in Calgary, Canada on October 19, 1918 but nine years later the family returned to Britain. At the age of 13 Bazalgette was diagnosed with tuberculosis but at the outbreak of war in 1939 he was deemed fit enough to enlist. He initially joined the Royal Artillery, serving in the Searchlight Section, but in 1941 he applied for a transfer to the RAF Volunteer Reserve (RAFVR). In September he was sent to RAF Cranwell, Lincolnshire for basic training and soloed after just a week of instruction.

Upon completing his basic training on January 24, 1942 he was promoted to the rank of Pilot Officer and passed through 15 OTU at RAF Finningley, Yorkshire before being declared ready for operations and allocated to 115 Sqn at RAF Mildenhall, Suffolk to fly Vickers Wellingtons on September 16.

Bazalgette flew 12 operations on the venerable Wellington before 115 Sqn were stood down at the end of November 1942 to train on the newly assigned Avro Lancasters. His first sortie on the new type was an aborted trip to St Nazaire in the Loire Valley in France on March 22, 1943 but four days later he and his crew conducted a successful 'visit' to Duisburg, Germany. Their Lancaster (DS615 – coded N) was badly damaged by flak and the loss of hydraulics meant Bazalgette was forced to belly

**Ian Willoughby Bazalgette, VC, DFC (October 19, 1918 – August 4, 1944)**

land back at base; hitting a tree in the process. Luckily nobody was injured and Bazalgette was awarded a DFC for his actions and general bravery in the face of the enemy.

Eight weeks later he was deemed to have flown the pre-requisite 30 missions (the majority in Lancasters) to complete his 'tour' and was promoted to Flight Commander and moved to RAF

Lossiemouth, Scotland to work as a flying instructor with 20 OTU.

Yearning for more operational flying, Bazalgette applied to join the RAF's famed Pathfinder Force (PFF) and on April 20, 1944 he was allocated to 635 (Pathfinder) Sqn at RAF Downham Market, Norfolk as a Squadron Leader. He flew his first sortie with the unit on May 6 and throughout the D-Day period he and his crew played an instrumental part in keeping the German defences at bay.

Ian Bazalgette's 54th sortie took place on August 4, 1944 when he was part of a force of 61 Lancasters tasked with attacking a V-1 storage depot at Trossy St Maximin, north of Paris.

Bazalgette was joined aboard Lancaster ND811 (coded F2-T) by navigator Flt Lt Geoffrey Goddard, bomb aimer Flt Lt Ivan A Hibberd, wireless operator Flt Lt 'Chuck' Godfrey DFC; all of whom had served alongside him at Lossiemouth. They were accompanied by rear gunner Sgt Doug Cameron DFM (a former member of Flt Sgt Rawdon Hume Middleton's crew – see page 58), flight engineer Sgt George Turner and upper gunner Flt Sgt Vernon V Leeder.

Sqn Ldr Bazalgette's journey to northern France was uneventful but as the first aircraft began their bombing runs they were met with intense flak. Bazalgette was determined to drop his flares as accurately as possible and

**Ian Bazalgette's Pathfiner Lancaster B.VI was registered ND811 and wore 635 Sqn codes as F2-T**
*Andy Hay/www.flyingart.co.uk*

A total of 7,377 Lancasters were built during the war years. In Nanton, Alberta the Bomber Command Museum of Canada has painted Lancaster FM159 into the F2-T markings of Bazalgette's aircraft.

## " The bomber performed a perfect landing; but then exploded "

maintained a straight and level route through the barrage of shrapnel.

Within moments both starboard engines were alight and flames were licking the fuselage, causing the Lancaster's entire starboard wing to burn down to its framework. Inside the bomber Hibberd had had his shoulder and arm torn away and smoke started to incapacitate other crewmembers.

Bazalgette was able to release his marker flares shortly before the aircraft began a slow spin. Briefly he regained control but was unable to maintain altitude and ordered his crew to bale out at 1,000ft (305m). At this point Bazalgette must have decided to attempt a landing in order to save the injured Hibberd and Leeder.

Approaching the village of Senantes

witnesses claim to have seen the Lancaster turn towards an open field. The bomber performed a perfect landing; but then exploded. Hibberd, Leeder and Bazalgette all perished in the fire – the skipper was just 25 years old.

At the end of the war Sqn Ldr Bazalgette's valour finally came to light and on August 17, 1945 he was awarded a posthumous Victoria Cross. ❖

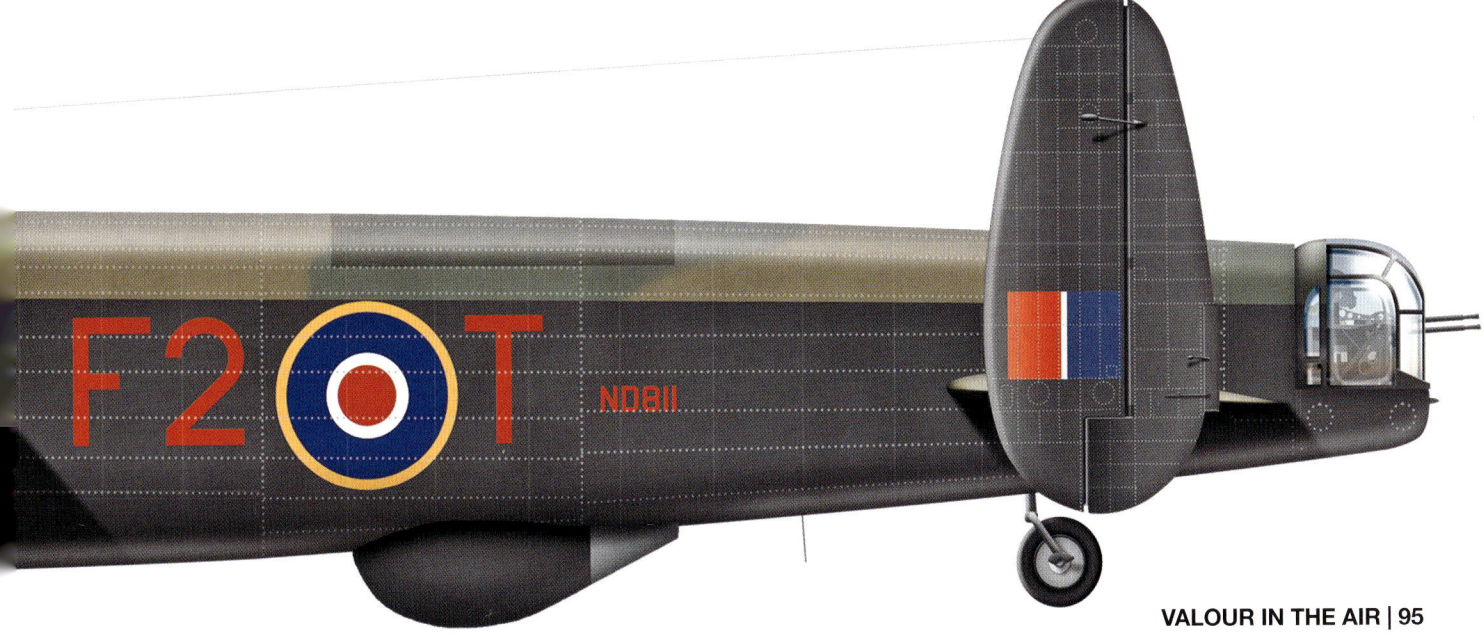

# The Philanthropic VC Holder

## As well as being awarded the VC, OM, DSO & Two Bars and DFC, 'Leonard' Cheshire became the RAF's youngest group captain but is perhaps best remembered for founding his post-war work concerning the care of the disabled

Geoffrey 'Leonard' Cheshire was born in Chester on September 7, 1917 but brought up near Oxford. He then studied law at Oxford University where he enjoyed the hedonistic lifestyle associated with the wealthy students of the era.

However, in 1937 developed an obsession for flying. He joined the Oxford University Air Squadron early that year; he had flown solo by June and on November 16 he received a commission as a pilot officer in the Royal Air Force Volunteer Reserve (RAFVR).

Cheshire fitted flying in alongside his studies until the outbreak of war when he was sent to 9 FTS at RAF Hullavington, Wiltshire to begin a permanent commission with the rank of Flying Officer.

At the end of further service training on June 6, 1940 Cheshire joined 102 Sqn at RAF Driffield, Yorkshire to fly the Armstrong Whitworth Whitley bomber. He flew numerous sorties over occupied Europe for the next few months and on the night of November 12/13 he was awarded a Distinguished Service Order (DSO) for bringing badly damaged Whitley P5005 safely back from a

**Geoffrey Leonard Cheshire, Baron Cheshire VC, OM, DSO & Two Bars, DFC (September 7, 1917 –July 31, 1992)**

mission from Cologne despite a 70kt (80mph) headwind.

In January 1941 Cheshire completed his 'tour' of 30 missions and immediately volunteered to fly another. He was posted to 35 Sqn at RAF Linton-on-Ouse, Yorkshire to fly the Handley Page

Halifax bomber. In March 1941 Cheshire was awarded the Distinguished Flying Cross (DFC) and was promoted to the war substantive rank of Flight Lieutenant on April 7. He was also presented with a 'Bar' to his DSO for 'outstanding leadership.'

By October Cheshire had completed a second full tour and had been promoted again, this time to Squadron Leader. He then transferred to 1652 Heavy Conversion Unit (HCU) at RAF Marston Moor, Yorkshire to instruct on the Halifax and despite being a 'non operational' unit he still managed to fly four trips to Germany, including as part of the first 1,000 bomber raids.

A second Bar was added to his DSO in April 1942 and in August he joined 76 Sqn at Linton-on-Ouse as the unit's commanding officer; a role he continued until he moved back to Marston Moor as base commander. This job came with yet another promotion: to Group Commander. And in March 1943, at the age of 25 Cheshire was the youngest RAF officer to ever hold such a post. However, he hated the office-based nature of the job and in September 1943 returned to a flying role to command the now-famous 617 'Dambusters' Sqn.

Cheshire was awarded a Distinguished Service Order (DSO) for bringing a badly damaged Whitley safely back from a mission over Cologne despite a 70kt headwind

During his time on 617 Sqn Cheshire was successful in convincing the authorities to replace Lancaster pathfinders with higher speed Mosquitos and Mustangs

## 'Leonard' Cheshire

An exponent of low-level attacks, Cheshire was initially frustrated at the order to teach his new squadron the art of high level bombing and even after four months of training with 617 Sqn he was convinced that the practice was out-dated. Therefore, when the order came to attack the Gnome-Rhone factory in Limoges, France on February 8, 1944 he defied instructions and marked the target from a mere 200ft (61m). With the target accurately highlighted the other bombers were able to drop their munitions exactly where they needed to – Cheshire's plan had been vindicated.

Faced with such a visible demonstration of the technique the higher ranks had little choice but to accept Cheshire's request for high speed de Havilland Mosquitos and then North American P-51 Mustangs to act as Pathfinders.

Grp Capt Cheshire continued to lead 617 Sqn's sorties over occupied Europe

**During his time flying the Halifax Cheshire was awarded the Distinguished Flying Cross and was presented with a 'Bar' to his DSO for 'outstanding leadership.'**

> ## " He flew his 100th operational sortie and was recommended for the Victoria Cross "

over the coming months and saw extensive action in the days immediately prior to and after D-Day. Then, on July 6, 1944, he flew his 100th operational sortie and was recommended for the Victoria Cross for his valour throughout his distinguished career to date.

In September 1944 he was despatched to the Far East to work with Eastern Air Command HQ in Calcutta, India and from there he transferred to the USA to join the British Joint Staff Mission in Washington DC. It was here that he was selected to observe the Atom bomb tests and in late July 1945 he flew back out to the Far East where he would subsequently be aloft in a Boeing B-29 Superfortress to witness the effects of the bomb dropped on Nagasaki, Japan on August 9.

The combined effect of more than 100 operational missions and what he saw that day in Japan resulted in Leonard Cheshire developing psychoneurosis and he was discharged from the RAF at his own request in January 1946. He had constantly been at war for almost six years.

In the post war years Cheshire created the VIP Colony (VIP standing for *Vade in Pacem* or Go in Peace) for veterans and war widows at Gumley Hall, Leicestershire to provide an opportunity for ex-servicemen and women and their families to live together to help their transition back into civilian life.

The following year he established the first Cheshire Foundation Home to support sick and disabled people. By

Cheshire's P-51B Mustang was coded HB837 and had the 'Malcolm' hood to improve visibility
*Andy Hay/www.flyingart.co.uk*

1955 there were six Cheshire homes in Britain and the first overseas home was built in Mumbai, India, a year later. Today there are more than 270 homes in 49 countries.

In the late 50s Leonard Cheshire met and married Sue Ryder, who had been a member of the Special Operations Executive in World War Two and gone on to form her own successful charities.

On July 31, 1992 Leonard Cheshire died of motor neurone disease at the age of 74. By then he had been made a life peer and was known as Baron Cheshire of Woodhall. His legacy will continue through the myriad of charities he formed or supported during his remarkable life. He was one of the most remarkable men of his generation, perhaps the most remarkable. ❖

# Transport Command's VC

**RAF Transport Command's only VC recipient lost his life in a manner many regard as one of the greatest individual acts of heroism of World War Two; this is David Lord's story**

The son of a Welsh Fusilier, David Samual Anthony Lord was born in Cork, Ireland on October 18, 1913 but the nature of his father's work meant he was schooled in India, England and Wales.

He was a shy and introvert young man whose first career aspiration was to enter the priesthood and to this end he attended the English Ecclesiastical College in Valladolid, Spain. However, he soon realised the church was not his vocation and he returned to Britain and worked as a freelance writer in both Wrexham and London.

Finally, on August 6, 1936 Lord enlisted as an airman in the RAF. It would be two more years before his application to become a pilot was approved and in October 1938 he moved to RAF Hamble, Hampshire for elementary training. After moving to 2

**David Samuel Anthony Lord VC, DFC (October 18, 1913 – September 19, 1944)**

FTS at RAF Brize Norton, Oxfordshire he was awarded his 'wings' on April 3, 1939 and sent to Lahore, India to join 31 Sqn as a Sergeant Pilot.

His first operational type was the veteran wood and fabric Vickers Valentia biplane and 31 Sqn used these to supply the various British Army units attempting to control India's North West Frontier Province (now Pakistan). The Valentia may have been out-dated but the outbreak of war in Europe meant re-equipping Indian-based units was not a priority and it would June 1941 before they were finally replaced with Douglas Dakotas.

Soon, the war effort in North Africa meant reinforcements were needed and 31 Sqn sent eight Dakotas and crew to support operations in Egypt and Libya. Among those crews was David Lord.

He flew extensively in the North

The RAF Dakota force played an instrumental role in the D-Day landings and the eventual push through Europe and the Low Countries

African theatre but on December 8, 1941 – the day the USA entered the war – Lord was flying Dakota DG475 when it was 'bounced' by a trio of Messerschmitt Bf109s. Although he was slightly wounded he managed to make a successful forced landing in the open desert without injuring his nine passengers or damaging the 1,500lb (680kg) of cargo. He then led the 10-mile (16km) walk to safety and returned to operational flying the following day.

In February 1942 Lord returned to India and three months later was promoted to the rank of Pilot Officer. He then continued to support the war effort against Japan in Burma and on July 16, 1943 was awarded a DFC for his continued bravery.

After completing four years of continuous operational flying Lord returned to Britain in January 1944 and was promoted to Flight Lieutenant. After a brief period of home leave he was soon posted to 271 Sqn at RAF Down Ampney, Gloucestershire where he began training to tow gliders in advance of the imminent Allied invasion of Europe.

On the night of June 5/6, 1944 Lord and his crew played an active role in the D-Day landings dropping paratroopers 6 miles (9.6km) north east of Caen as part of Operation *Neptune*. Despite his Dakota being significantly

On the night of June 5/6, 1944 Lord and his crew played an active role in the D-Day landings dropping paratroopers 6 miles north east of Caen as part of Operation *Neptune*

An aerial view of the Arnhem Bridge, which was eventually captured by Allied forces as they advanced eastwards in 1944

damaged by flak, with holes in the rudder, elevator and hydraulics, Lord got his 'passengers' safely to the target and returned home ready for his next sortie. For the next two weeks he and his colleagues flew a succession of supply drops over the beachhead and during the coming months they carried out a number of support flights for the advancing troops.

Two months later David Lord and his crew would also take part in the Battle of Arnhem as part of Operation *Market Garden*. They flew their first sorties on September 17 and met little resistance from the German forces in the Netherlands and the Low Countries. However, the following day Lord was towing an Airspeed Horsa glider full of troops when his Dakota came under a hail of flak fire. The rear fuselage of his aircraft was badly damaged by shrapnel but he was undeterred and the following day he returned to the same area.

September 19 dawned cloudy and foggy forcing a postponement to 271 Sqn's launch from Down Ampney but by 1.00pm the weather had improved sufficiently to take off. That day David Lord was flying Dakota III KG374 – coded YS-DM – but most of his regular crew were unavailable to join him. Navigator F/O MacDonnell had gone on leave to get married and was replaced by F/O Harry King and P/O

## " King was thrown from the aircraft door and barely had time to pull the ripcord before he hit the ground "

'Dickie' Medhurst stood in for second pilot F/O Ager. Only Lord's regular wireless operator F/O Alec Ballantyne was available that day and the 'stand-in' crew were joined by despatchers Cpl Philip Nixon and Privates Leonard Harder, Jimmy Ricketts and Arthur Rowbotham.

Seventeen Dakotas launched into the grey skies loaded with ammunition panniers destined for Drop Zone (DZ) 'V' on the outskirts of Arnhem; however, unbeknown to the allies, the DZ was already in German hands.

To make matters worse, a timing error meant the Dakotas failed to meet up with their fighter escort. Ten miles (16km) from the DZ Lord descended through the cloud and broke clear at 1,500ft (457m) above the River Rhine at 3.07pm.

Almost immediately the Dakota was engaged by an intense battery of flak and the starboard engine burst into flames. The radar was also destroyed but Lord decided to press on toward Arnhem and intended to drop the load visually.

Three minutes later KG374 passed over the target and Lord gave the despatchers the 'green light' to drop the cargo. At this point he also pressed the intercom switch and instructed everybody to be prepared in case they needed to bail out. Seconds later he turned on the 'red light' but learned that only half the panniers had been successfully dropped.

By now the Dakota was down to 900ft (274m) and the engine fire was starting to spread to the entire starboard wing. Undeterred, Lord swung the aircraft around in a steep turn to begin another pass over the DZ to allow the loadmasters another chance to loose their cargo. The aircraft was now descending through 600ft (183m) and subsequent reports from those on the ground stated that for a few seconds the fighting stopped as all eyes turned to the skies to watch the crew of the burning aeroplane attempting to complete their mission.

With the panniers finally released Lord gave the order to bail out. Harry King strapped on his parachute before

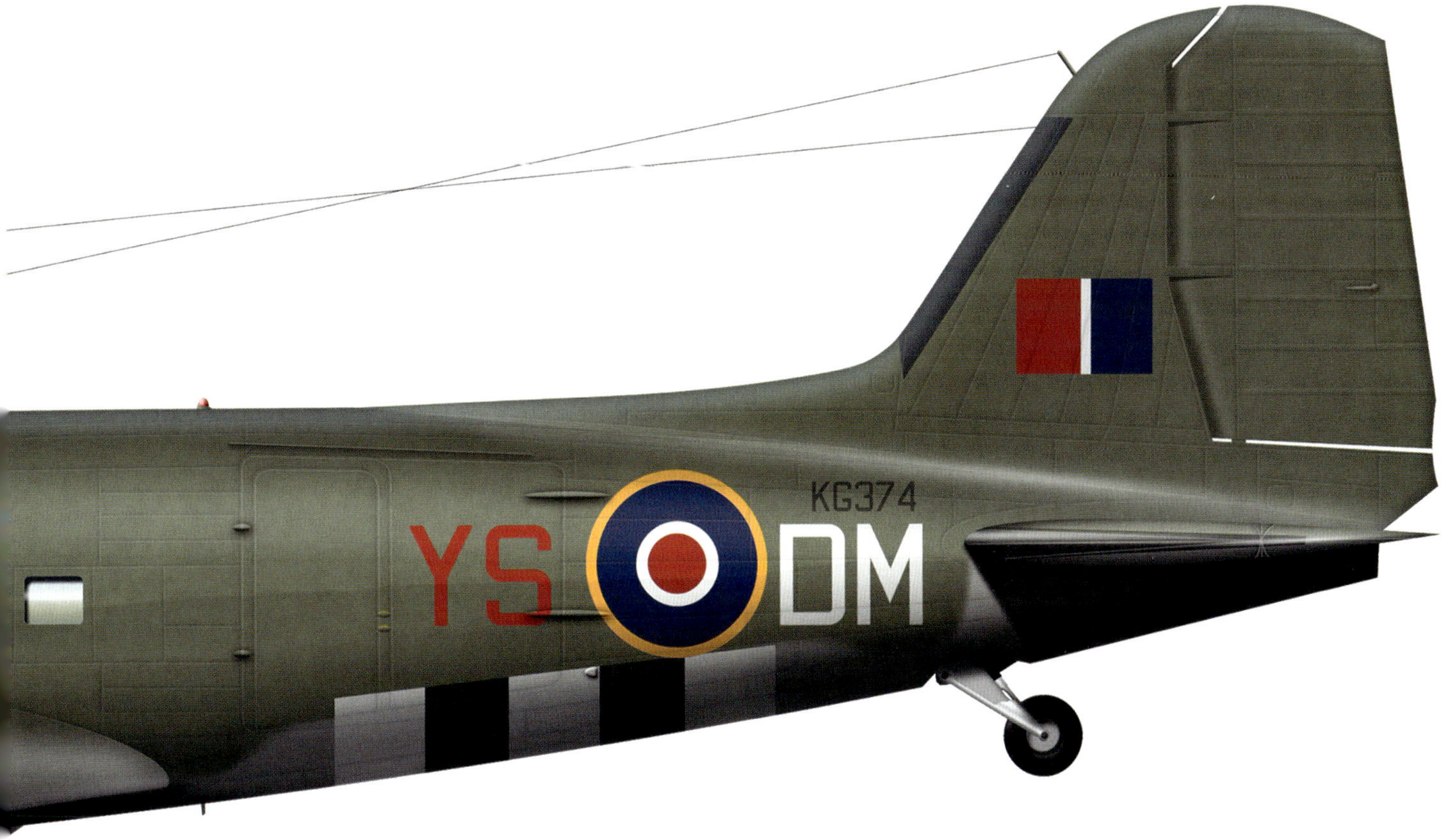

A number of preserved DC-3/C-47s have worn the markings of KG374, including this example at the RAF Museum, Cosford, Shropshire. It is really KN645 and has since been repainted into a post-war scheme and hangs from the ceiling of the National Cold War Museum

beginning to help the despatchers with theirs, but seconds later there was an enormous 'crack' as the burning wing separated from the fuselage. At that moment King was thrown from the aircraft door and he barely had time to pull the ripcord before he hit the ground, hard but alive. Looking up he saw the Dakota crash in a ball of flames. Still aboard were Lord,

Ballantyne, Medhurst and the four Army despatchers – none of them would survive. It was 3.16pm – just nine minutes after the aircraft had first been hit.

King spent the night fighting alongside troops from the Parachute Regiment but at 9.00am the next morning he was captured by the Germans and spent the remainder of

the war as a POW.

After VE Day, King was repatriated to Britain on May 13, 1945 and it was at this point that David Lord's amazing gallantry finally became known. The 'skipper' was awarded a posthumous Victoria Cross on November 13 and his parents received their son's medal at Buckingham Palace on December 18. ❖

# Aviation was in his Blood

**Sqn Ldr Palmer was lost on his 111th operational mission. His citation noted that he was "an outstanding pilot" who "displayed conspicuous bravery" and "his record of prolonged and heroic endeavour is beyond praise." This is his story.**

The son of ex-Royal Flying Corps pilot Arthur Palmer, Robert Anthony Maurice Palmer was born in Gillingham, Kent on July 7, 1920. With aviation running through his blood from a young age it would be inevitable that he soon became an aeromodeller with aspirations to become a pilot.

However, on his father's advice, he joined the Surveyors' department at Gravesend Borough Council upon leaving school. The outbreak of war in 1939 gave him the 'excuse' to follow his dream and on August 22 of that year he enlisted in the RAF Volunteer Reserves (RAFVR).

Flying instruction began on September 25 with 3 Initial Training Wing (ITW) at Hastings, Sussex and, later, ETFS at Desford near Leicester. In June 1940 Palmer transferred to 12 FTS at Grantham, Lincolnshire and he graduated as a Sergeant Pilot on September 7.

After a period with 15 OTU at Harwell, Berkshire he reported to his first operational unit – 75 Sqn at Feltwell, Norfolk – on November 16.

Sgt Plt 'Bob' Palmer only stayed with 75 Sqn for ten days but flew three operational sorties over Germany as a second pilot on Vickers Wellingtons during that time. On November 26 he was transferred to 149 Sqn at Mildenhall, Suffolk where he had completed a full tour of 30 missions on Wellingtons by February 13, 1941.

At this point he was promoted to Flight Sergeant and moved to 20 OTU at

**Robert Anthony Maurice Palmer VC DFC (July 7, 1920 – December 23, 1944)**

RAF Lossiemouth, Scotland to work as a flying instructor. A further promotion (to Pilot Officer) followed in January 1942 but various requests to return to a squadron were repeatedly declined.

It was only the introduction of the first '1,000 bomber raid' in early 1942 – and the need for 'all hands on deck' – that Palmer was finally granted permission to return to operational flying. He flew in three such raids in May and June before returning to instructional duties and receiving more promotions; resulting in him being a Flight Lieutenant by the end of the year.

The following year he met Ian

Bazalgette [see page 94], who was also instructing at Lossiemouth and agreed to lend his support to Palmer's latest application for a transfer. Finally, he got what he wanted and on November 9, 1943 he was transferred to the Pathfinder Force (PFF) to train on the de Havilland Mosquito with 109 Sqn at Marham, Norfolk. True to the PFF ethos Palmer made a name for himself flying low level, precision missions to 'mark' targets for other squadrons and he quickly completed a second tour. On June 30, 1944 he was awarded the DFC in view of his continued bravery and skill but, to the amazement of his colleagues, he then volunteered for a third tour and on December 8 he completed his 100th operational sortie. This gave the young pilot another opportunity to 'retire' but yet again he opted to stay with the PFF – this time as a Squadron Leader with a 'Bar' added to his DFC.

He flew several more missions that month and on December 23 he and his crew were preparing for his 111th mission. The target for the day was the Gremburg marshalling yards near Cologne, Germany – a daylight mission to be flown by 27 Avro Lancasters and three Mosquitos drawn from 35, 105, 109 and 582 Sqns; all of which were PFF units.

Palmer was designated 'Master Bomber' for the mission and using 'Oboe' radar bombing equipment he would mark the targets for the other heavy bombers to aim for.

Instead of his usual Mosquito, Sqn Ldr Palmer 'borrowed' a 582 Sqn

Palmer regularly flew Pathfinder Force missions in Mosquitos but on the mission that cost him his life he opted to fly a borrowed Lancaster

The successes of Bomber Command were purchased at terrible cost. Of every 100 airmen who joined Bomber Command, 45 were killed, 6 were seriously wounded, 8 became Prisoners of War, and only 41 escaped unscathed (at least physically)

Lancaster (PB371 – coded 60-V) for this sortie and in addition to his usual navigator, Flt Lt George Russell DFC, he also took along a highly experienced crew of 582 Sqn men. Flt Lt Owen Milne DFC would act as second pilot and Sqn Ldr Albert Carter DFC would perform second navigator duties. They would be joined by signals operator Flt Sgt 'Bert' Nundy, mid-upper gunner F/O William

Dalgarno and tail gunner W/O Yeulatt.

Palmer eased the heavily loaded Lancaster off the runway at Little Staughton, Bedfordshire at 10.27am quickly followed by Lancaster PB120 (60-P) flown by Flt Lt Walter Reif, who was due to complete his first operational tour with the trip.

They soon joined the other aircraft but as they coasted out over the

Thames Estuary two of the 27 Lancaster collided, resulting in the loss of all 14 aboard.

The remainder of the flight to Germany proved uneventful but the 10/10 cloud forecast by the 'met men' failed to materialise and as they approached the target at 17,000ft (5,182m) clear blue skies gave the flak gunners ideal shooting conditions.

Ignoring the sky full of shrapnel Palmer maintained the prolonged straight and steady run in towards the target necessary to drop the weapons accurately. However, shells were soon hitting the airframe with frightening regularity and two engines were soon on fire.

Palmer could easily have turned for safety but he knew the following bombers needed him to accurately mark the target so he continued flying the blazing bomber towards the target until he received the radar release signal.

No sooner had he called "bombs gone" than the stricken bomber rolled onto its back and spiralled down to earth. Only the tail gunner escaped.

Behind, Reif's Lancaster took a direct flak hit in the bomb bay and burst into flames. He ordered his crew to bail out and only two of his men escaped before the bomber crashed into the centre of Cologne and exploded.

Of the 30 aircraft launched that day eight failed to return and all the remainder were damaged to one degree or another.

At the time of his death, on his 111th mission, 'Bob' Palmer was just 24 years old. He was awarded a posthumous VC on March 23, 1945; the citation noting "He displayed conspicuous bravery. His record of prolonged and heroic endeavour is beyond praise." ❖

The Lancaster Palmer was flying on the mission that earned him a posthumous VC was registered PB371 and wore the 582 Sqn codes 60-V

*Andy Hay/www.flyingart.co.uk*

# "Young in Years but with Actions of a Veteran"

**When George Thompson's Lancaster was hit by flak the apprentice grocer turned wireless operator went to the aid of his mid upper gunner, using his bare hands to extinguish flames in an attempt to rescue his comrade. This is his amazing story**

The son of a Scottish ploughman, George Thompson was born in Trinity Gask, Perthshire on October 23, 1920. He left school at 15 and began working as an apprentice grocer but shortly after qualifying he volunteered to join the military to 'do his bit' and help the war effort.

After a period with the Local Defence Volunteers in Kinross he requested to join the RAF Volunteer Reserves (RAFVR) in January 1941. Although he was rejected for aircrew training he was successful in receiving a posting as ground crew.

A boyhood interest in all things electrical stood him in good stead and he was chosen to train as a ground-based wireless operator before being sent to Iraq. However, he soon became bored and, wanting to play a more active role in the fighting, applied again to become a member of aircrew.

This time Thompson was accepted and arrived back in Britain in August 1943 to begin training as an air wireless operator. He graduated on November 29 and then attended an air gunnery school before being sent to 14 OTU at Market Harborough, Leicestershire.

While at the OTU he was recruited by New Zealand-born Harry Denton to join 'his' crew. Thompson would be the wireless operator and he would fly alongside bomb aimer Ron Goebel, navigator Ted Kneebone and air gunners Haydn Price and Ernest 'Ernie' Potts.

After a number of practice sorties flying Vickers Wellingtons the new crew

**George Thompson VC
(October 23, 1920 - January 23, 1945)**

then went to the Heavy Conversion Unit (HCU) to fly the Short Stirling and it would here that they would add Wilf Hartshorn to their group. Soon they were sent on the Avro Lancaster conversion course and were then posted to 9 Sqn at Bardney, Lincolnshire. They flew their first operational sortie on October 6, 1944 and by the end of November Thompson had been promoted to the rank of Flight Sergeant.

During the squadron's New Year's Eve celebrations Denton's crew were informed that they needed to moderate their alcohol intake as they were flying a short-notice mission at dawn. The target would be the heavily defended Dortmund-Ems Canal.

Denton's men were allocated Lancaster PD377 – coded WS-U – for the mission and it was loaded with a dozen 1,000lb (454kg) high explosive bombs. The Lancaster lifted off just before 7.45am as the first of a ten-ship take off. The heavy aircraft lumbered into the skies and as he turned onto track Denton looked over his shoulder and saw the second and third Lancasters crashing in flames next to the runway.

Undeterred, Denton pressed on with the mission and met up with 100 other bombers from 5 Group over northern France before making their run in towards the target at 10,000ft.

Although the flak was intense PD377 managed to reach the target unscathed and successfully dropped its bombs before turning to head home to England. However, shortly afterwards, their luck ran out and an 88mm (3.5in) shell smashed into the Lancaster's nose where Goebel had been kneeling. The explosion ripped open the top off the aircraft's Plexiglas canopy and also set the number 2 engine alight.

Almost simultaneously a second shell entered the bottom of the fuselage, severing the control cables and hydraulic lines as well as causing a fire that engulfed the upper gun turret where Ernie Potts was sitting.

The air rushing in the now 'open' cockpit was feeding the fire further aft and the navigator also watched helplessly as his maps and charts were sucked out through the gaping hole. Amazingly, moments later a blackened and dazed but uninjured Goebel appeared from the nose carrying the torn remains of his parachute pack.

Meanwhile, George Thompson realised that both gun turrets were now alight and the gunners trapped in their seats. Even though he was not wearing gloves, a parachute or any protective clothing the wireless operator began to head towards the flames. Reaching the hole in the fuselage floor he had to hold onto the hot metal skin with his finger tips then, having successfully traversed the obstacle he removed the now unconscious Potts from his turret and used his bare hands to extinguish the gunner's clothes, which were by

**A 'typical' Lancaster bomb load comprising of a 4,000lb 'Cookie' blast bomb and 12 Small Bomb Containers, each with 236 x 4lb incendiary bombs**

**Ground crew prepare a Lancaster for the night's mission over occupied Europe**

now well alight. Even though his own flying suit was now on fire Thompson lifted the gunner onto his shoulder and carried him back across the gaping hole to relative safety.

The wireless operator then turned his attention to Haydn Price, the tail gunner. Retracing his perilous route through the disintegrating fuselage he reached the tail turret and knocked on the door. Price had already tried to bail out but had been beaten back by the intense flames surrounding the tail and when he opened the door he was amazed to see his friend standing there, singed and blackened.

Thompson guided Price to safety by which time his own face was blistering from the heat and flames and his clothes had all but burned away. Yet he was still concerned that the pilot might order a bailout without realising that the injured gunner could not fend for himself. Consequently Thompson fought his way through even more flames to reach the flight deck and give a report on what had happened.

By now Denton had his hands full flying a badly damaged aircraft and shortly after received Thompson's information the Lancaster was hit by even more flak. This time the number 3 engine was hit and the aircraft began to descend at a rapid rate.

As Denton passed through 5,000ft (1,524m) he was shocked to see a flight of German fighters flash past his cockpit hotly pursued by a group of Spitfires. Spotting that the Lancaster was in trouble the Spitfire pilots broke off their chase and joined formation with the bomber in an attempt to guide it to their own airfield. But the Lancaster was in no state to fly that far and Denton began to let it down into a field. It was then that one of the Spitfires 'cut him up' in an attempt to warn him about high voltage cables ahead of the aircraft; Dalton was able to haul the aircraft over the wires and then he noticed a village dead ahead. The aircraft had just enough flying speed to make a slight turn and second later it bellied into a grass field. The airframe broke in two and the crew – including Potts who had now regained consciousness – were able to scramble to safety.

As they gathered under the safety of a nearby hedge the horrendously burned Thompson turned to Denton, smiled, and said: "Jolly good landing Skipper!"

The Spitfire pilots had radioed through the location of the 'landing' and soon an ambulance was on the scene to take the crew to the nearby hospital at Eindhoven Castle.

Upper gunner Ernie Potts later succumbed to his injuries but tail gunner Haydn Price made a full recovery – his life saved by the bravery of 24-year-old wireless operator George Thompson.

Thompson himself began to make a good recovery, despite his terrible burns, and was reportedly a model patient. He remained cheerful and never complained but 13 days later he developed pneumonia and passed away. The award of his posthumous Victoria Cross was announced on February 20 with the citation noting that while he was "young in years and experience, his actions were those of a veteran." ❖

**The Avro Lancaster B.1 George Thompson was flying aboard was registered PD377 and wore the WS-U codes of 9 Sqn**

# South Africa's VC

## The only South African pilot to receive a VC during World War Two was Ted Swales; this is the story of how he sacrificed himself to save his men

Edwin 'Ted' Essery Swales was born into a farming family in Inanda, Natal, South Africa on July 3, 1915 but lost his father to influenza when he was just three years of age.

He finished his schooling and in 1934 joined Barclays Bank's Dominion Colonial and Overseas office in Durban while maintaining a keen interest in sports into adulthood; excelling at both rugby and cricket.

In 1935 he enlisted in the Natal Mounted Rifles (similar to Britain's Territorial Army) and at the outbreak of war in 1939 he was mobilised and sent to fight in Abyssinia (now Ethiopia), Kenya and in the North Africa campaign before transferring to the South African Air Force on January 17, 1942.

Accepted for pilot training he began learning to fly at 75 Air School at Lyttleton, near Pretoria on February 2. A year later, on February 23, 1943, he began advanced conversion training on twin-engined Airspeed Oxfords at 21 Air School at Kimberley in the North Cape region and was finally awarded his wings on June 26.

In August of that year Swales was given a choice of duties; he could either remain in his native country as an instructor or head to Europe to fly operationally with the RAF. Without hesitation he opted to join Bomber Command and was immediately

**Edwin (Ted) Essery Swales VC DFC (July 3, 1915 – February 23, 1945)**

seconded to the RAF before sailing to Britain aboard the *Rangitata* along with 60 other pilots.

Upon arrival he was attached to 6 AFU at Little Rissington, Gloucestershire to fly both Oxfords and Avro Ansons prior to joining 83 OTU at Peplow, Shropshire for conversion onto the Vickers Wellington bomber. Further training included a period with the night training unit of the Pathfinder Force (PFF), the Lancaster OTU and then, in

early July 1944, he finally joined his first operational squadron – 582 Sqn at Little Staughton, Bedfordshire.

Ted Swales' first sortie with the squadron occurred on July 12 when he flew Lancaster PB149 to Thiverny in Northern France and back. On his fourth mission he diverted to land at the Handley Page airfield at Radlet, but misjudged his landing at this unfamiliar site and crashed. He suffered concussion but the rest of the crew escaped unhurt. He was flying operational missions again five nights later.

He continued flying regular missions but in October he was shot down and belly-landed safely near Brussels without injury to himself or his crew. By the following month he had been promoted to Captain and on December 23 he flew as 'number 2' to Sqn Ldr 'Bob' Palmer on the mission that earned the latter his posthumous VC (see p104). Soon after Palmer had been shot down Swales found himself under heavy attack by fighters so he swung his Lancaster round so as to give his gunners the best chance to retaliate. Despite five waves of attack by the fighters Swales gunners destroyed one aircraft and damaged two more. For his coolness Swales was awarded the DFC.

On January 1, 1945 Swales was promoted and flew his first sortie as 'Master Bomber'; leading a mission

**Ted Swales with his crew prior to strapping into Lancaster III PB538/60-M ready for their trip to Pforzheim, Germany**

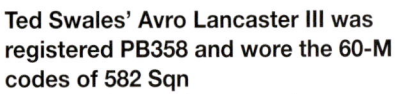

**Ted Swales' Avro Lancaster III was registered PB358 and wore the 60-M codes of 582 Sqn**

*Andy Hay/www.flyingart.co.uk*

For most of the war, the majority of those who entered Bomber Command did not survive. Of those who flew with Bomber Command at the beginning of the war, only 10% survived the conflict. It is a loss rate comparable only to the worst slaughter of the First World War trenches, and only the Nazi U-Boat force suffered a higher casualty rate

against Nuremburg in which he bravely circled the target for a lengthy period to ensure the main bomber force had bombed accurately.

By February 23 Ted Swales had flown 42 operational sorties and that evening he and his crewmembers strapped into Lancaster III PB538 – coded 60-M – ready for a trip to Pforzheim, Germany. Swales was to again act as Master Bomber for this mission and he was flying with his regular crew: Sqn Ldr D Archer DSO DFC (navigator), P/O R Wheaton (2nd navigator), Flt Lt Clive Dodson DSO, DFC (bomb aimer) Flt Sgt George Bennington DFM (flight engineer), P/O A V Goodacre (wireless operator) Flt Sgt B Leach (dorsal gunner) and P/O N Bourne (tail gunner).

The Lancaster lifted off from Little Staughton at 4.36pm and the flight to Germany passed without incident. Then, just as they arrived over the target, PB358 was attacked by a Messerschmitt Bf 110 night fighter, which hit the Number 3 engine, wing fuel tanks and destroyed Bourne's tail turret. Swales checked in with his

crew and upon hearing that, amazingly, nobody was injured decided to press on with the attack on just three engines. He dropped his target markers and then circled the target to give radio instructions to the following bombers – effectively making himself a sitting duck as he was silhouetted against the glow of the target indicators he had just dropped.

Eventually another night fighter appeared and raked Swales' Lancaster with cannon fire. This time the Number 2 engine was destroyed and the fuselage was peppered with holes. By now Swales was struggling to maintain altitude and was down to just 4,000ft (1,219m) but still he insisted on circling the target to direct the attack.

Only when he was satisfied that the target had been destroyed did Ted Swales finally turn for home. Despite the lack of power, sluggish controls and low airspeed the captain was determined to make it back to England; specifically the RAF base at Manston, Kent – just across the English Channel. However, it soon became apparent

that Kent was beyond the range of the battered bomber and Swales' new objective became getting the aircraft back beyond Allied lines.

Eventually, as they passed overhead Limburg, Belgium, the wallowing Lancaster could no longer remain clear of the bubbling, turbulent cumulus clouds and as it slipped into their peaks it quickly became almost un-flyable. Next the two remaining engines began to overheat and produce even less power and finally the rudder controls sheared and PB358 entered a slow flat spin. Swales ordered his men to bail out as he tried with all his strength to keep the Lancaster from turning on its back.

As the seven men floated down beneath their silk parachutes the sky lit up as the Lancaster crashed and exploded beneath them. Twenty nine year old Ted Swales was still aboard. He had sacrificed himself for his friends. For his selfless valour he was awarded a posthumous Victoria Cross on April 24, 1945. He was the only member of the South African Air Force to receive the honour. ❖

# The Final Airborne VC (To Date...)

**Robert Gray was the sixth Canadian but only the second member of the Fleet Air Arm to receive the VC. He was also the final person to be awarded the medal during World War Two and the most recent aviator so decorated. This is how he carved his name into history**

Robert Hampton 'Hammy' Gray was born in British Columbia, Canada on November 2, 1917 as the son of a jeweller and following his schooling he attended the University of British Columbia to study for an arts degree.

As soon as he graduated in 1940 he volunteered to join the Royal Canadian Naval Volunteer Reserve and enlisted as an Ordinary Seaman on August 3 of that year. Gray was soon selected for pilot training and sent to Britain by liner. On his arrival, in December, he was given orders to report to the HMS *St Vincent* ground station in Gosport, Hampshire and by October 1941 he had been awarded his wings and promoted to Sub Lieutenant. Postings to HMS *Daedulus* (Lee-on-Solent, Hampshire) and HMS *Heron* (Yeovilton, Somerset) followed for more training followed and then, on March 10, 1942, he transferred to his first operational Squadron: 757 NAS at HMS *Kestrel* (Worthy Down, Hampshire).

By May 1942 the young pilot, still only 25 years old, had been moved to 789 NAS and assigned to the North African theatre where he flew shore-based Hawker Hurricanes from bases in Kenya.

It would be May 1944 before Gray finally left Africa and following a few weeks' home leave in Canada he returned to Britain where he was appointed to 1841 Sqn aboard the aircraft carrier HMS *Formidable* to fly the big Chance Vought Corsair fighter.

In July and August 1944 the carrier was sailing in the waters around Norway and 'Hammy' Gray flew as part of several missions against the German battleship *Tirpitz*. On August 29 he flew his Corsair in support of yet another mission against the 823ft (251m) long battleship and although cloud and fog obscured their objective he and his squadron mates pressed on through a barrage of flak. Flying ahead of *Formidable's* Fairey Barracuda bomber Gray led a flight of Corsairs to strafe the anti-aircraft defences; on one occasion leading his section on a low-level strike against three heavily armed destroyers. His own gun camera footage showed he had flown directly at the guns of one

**Robert Hampton 'Hammy' Gray, VC, DSC (November 2, 1917 – August 9, 1945)**

of the ships and attacked the bridge with great precision; gallantry which resulted in the brave Canadian earning a 'Mention in Despatches.'

With the sea war all but over in Europe by April 1945 HMS *Formidable* was sent to the Pacific to continue

the fight against the Japanese as the British fleet moved northwards towards Okinawa. Once again 'Hammy' Gray conducted various successful air strikes against both enemy shipping and airfields and on July 28 he scored a direct hit on a destroyer, causing the Japanese vessel to sink. This, combined with his remarkable career to date, resulted in him being awarded the Distinguished Service Order (DSO).

In early August the British carrier stood down for replenishment and during this time the US forces dropped the first atomic bomb on Hiroshima, Japan on August 6, 1945. HMS *Formidable* was due to return to action on August 8 but a typhoon in the area meant the aircraft were unable to fly. It was therefore August 9 before Robert Gray was able to return to the battle; flying one of three 'Ramrod' fighter sweeps 1841Sqn had been tasked with flying against Japanese airfields that day.

Flying Corsair KD658 – coded 115 – Gray took off from the carrier's deck shortly after 8.00am leading a flight of seven other Corsairs. They climbed to

**Robert Gray's Fleet Air Arm Corsair IV was registered KD658 and coded 115**
*Andy Hay/www.flyingart.co.uk*

The Vintage Wings of Canada collection in Gatineau, Quebec has painted Corsair BuNo 92016 to represent the aircraft flown by 'Hammy' Gray on his final flight
*Doug Fisher*

10,000ft (3,048m) and headed for the Japanese mainland. Each aircraft was loaded with a pair of 500lb (227kg) high explosive bombs in addition to their usual four wing mounted .50in machine guns and the briefing called for them to make just a single pass over the enemy airfield that had been designated as the primary target.

The eight Corsairs made landfall after a 150 mile (241km) flight from the ship and as he crossed the coast Gray immediately noted a pair of Japanese destroyers and various escort vessels anchored in the Onagawa Wan (Bay) near Miyagi Prefecture, Japan.

As he arrived over the target airfield Gray looked down in dismay to find that it had already been struck by other Allied aircraft. He saw no point in

wasting bombs on an already disabled airfield so he radioed his colleagues and told them to switch their attention to the ships in the bay.

Although they were still at 10,000ft (3,048m) their arrival was masked by the surrounding hills and when the ships came into sight all eight fighters began a simultaneous 400mph (348kt) dive to begin their attack. However, the ships' gunners must already have seen the Corsairs cruise overhead minutes earlier and as soon as the fighters appeared over the hilltops all hell broke loose as every possible anti-aircraft gun opened fire at the same time. Each ship had a myriad of defensive guns and the surrounding hills were also bristling with weaponry and within second the sky was full of flak and tracer.

Undeterred, Gray continued to lead the assault and descended to just 40ft (12m) above the waves before dropping his two bombs on the Etorofu-class escort ship *Amakusa*.

From start to finish the entire attack lasted not more than 20 seconds, but when the sky had cleared Gray was nowhere to be seen. His Corsair's port wing had exploded under a hail of fire and the fighter plunged into the water.

Sub Lt MacKinnon now took command of the flight of seven remaining aircraft, which circled the bay and began a second attack. It was then that they noted the *Amakusa* had already sunk; evidence later showing that 71 of her 150 men went down with the ship. The Corsairs managed to damage two more ships on their second pass and then the crews made their way back to HMS *Formidable* to break the news that their beloved friend and colleague had been killed.

Robert Hampton Gray was just 27 years old when he died and on November 13, 1945 he became the sixth Canadian to be awarded the Victoria Cross – albeit posthumously. He had survived five years of war only to be killed within a few days of the ultimate Allied Victory.

To date, he remains the last aviator to be awarded the highest award of the British honours system. The VC is presented for gallantry "in the face of the enemy", and that is something that 'Hammy' Gray possessed in spades. ❖

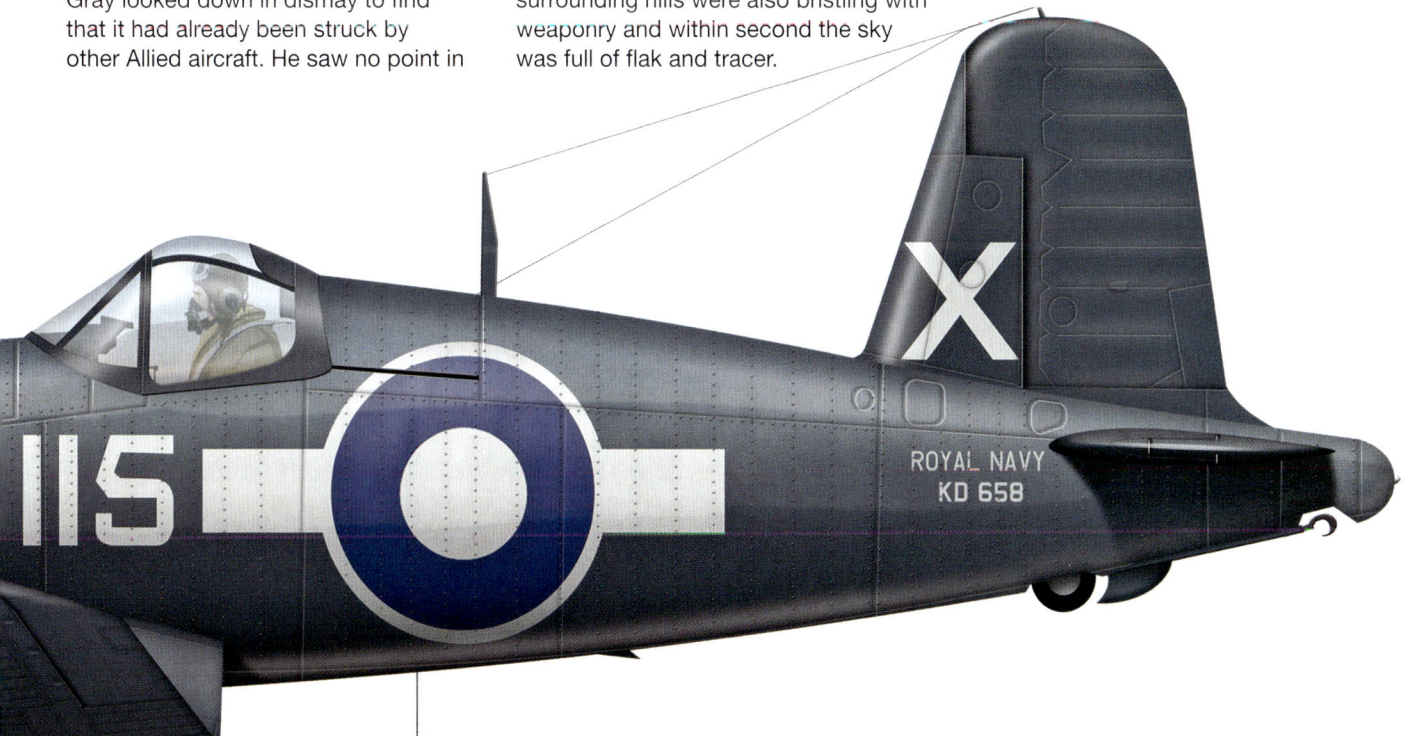

**❝ All hell broke loose as every possible anti-aircraft gun opened fire at the same time ❞**

# Recognising the Gallant Few

## It is now 75 years since a Victoria Cross was last awarded to an aviator. However, the 51 recipients are far from forgotten and their legacy lives on

The 51 brave aviators who have been awarded the Victoria Cross represent less than 4% of the total 1,358 medals presented since 1857.

Although Commonwealth airmen have been involved in various wars and conflicts over the past 70 years the changing style of aerial warfare has meant that no VCs have been awarded to flyers since Robert Hampton-Gray in August 1945 (see page 110).

In fact, the changing face of warfare in general has meant that just 15 VCs have been awarded in total since the end of World War Two; these being four presented in the Korean War, a single one in the Indonesia-Malaysia confrontation in 1965, four to Australians in the Vietnam War, two during the Falklands War in 1982, one in the Iraq War in 2004, and three in Afghanistan between 2006 and 2012.

### Medals For Sale

The first sale of a recipient's VC took place in 1879 and since then more than 300 of the medals have been sold, either publicly or privately.

Over the years the 'value' of a Victoria Cross has grown exponentially. A medal belonging to the family of Surgeon Major Edmund Barron Hartley (awarded for service during the Basuto Gun War in 1879) was sold in 1955 for a then-record of £500 (around £12,600 in today's money) but just eleven years later the Middlesex Regiment paid a new record figure of £900 (approximately £16,000 today) for a VC awarded after the Battle of the Somme.

In November 2009, the medal awarded to William Reid fetched £384,000 at auction - over £520,000 at 2020 rates. It later transpired that his sister, Melissa John had outbid the buyers acting for the Lord Ashcroft Collection.

### Collections

In recent years a large proportion of medals sold at auction have been acquired by or for the Ashcroft Collection.

Founded in 1986 by British businessman and politician Lord Ashcroft the collection now contains 162 medals (around a tenth of all VCs awarded) and is now the largest collection of such decorations.

The RAF's Vickers VC10 fleet carried the names of VC holders from the late 1960s until the type's eventual retirement in 2013 *Crown Copyright*

In July 2008 Lord Ashcroft also donated £5 million to help fund a new permanent gallery at the Imperial War Museum (IWM) in London. The Lord Ashcroft Gallery opened in November 2010 and contains medals belonging to his own collection as well as those held by the IWM itself. A total of 210 VCs and 31 George Crosses are currently on display within the gallery.

Elsewhere, the largest collection outside the UK is held by the Australian War Memorial (AWM), whose display includes all nine VCs awarded to Australians at Gallipoli. The AWM holds 70 of the 100 VC medals awarded to Australians in all conflicts; including all three aircrew (Middleton, Newton and Ward).

In terms of aviation related VCs a total of 14 are held in the Ashcroft Collection and a further 11 are owned by the RAF Museum. The IWM holds three medals (Ferdinand West, Eugene Esmonde and Leonard Cheshire) and two are held in the Fleet Air Arm Museum.

### Honoured by the RAF

During their RAF service a number of Vickers VC10 tanker/transports bore the names of Victoria Cross recipients by way of a flying tribute.

The decision to name the first 14 aircraft was made by Wg Cdr Mike Beavis, who commanded 10 Sqn in the late 1960s.

However, with just 14 airframes available to pay tribute to 51 men some serious thought had to be given as to who should be recognised. The decision was therefore made to restrict the list to those who were born in the UK and flew operations within the RAF or RFC. This reduced the list to 21 names consisting of seven Great War pilots and 14 World War Two airmen. The latter included eight men from Bomber Command so it was decided to name one of the VC10s 'Guy Gibson' and allow this famous aviator to

---

## RAF VC10 Tributes

The following VC winning pilots lent their names to the RAF's fleet of Vickers VC10 tanker/transports for more than 40 years from the 1960s:

**George Thompson VC** (XR806 – later ZA148)
**Donald Garland** VC and **Thomas Gray** VC (XR807 – later ZA150)
**Kenneth Campbell** VC (XR808)
**Hugh Malcolm** VC (XR809 – later XR808)
**David Lord** VC (XR810 – later ZD241)
**Lanoe Hawker** VC (XV101 – later ZA150)
**Guy Gibson** VC (XV102 – later ZA148)
**Edward Mannock** VC (XV103 – later ZA149 & ZA147)
**James McCudden** VC (XV104 – later ZD241 & ZA147)
**Albert Ball** VC (XV105 – later ZA147)
**Thomas Mottershead** VC (XV106 – later XR808)
**James Nicolson** VC (XV107 – later ZA149 & ZA147)
**William Rhodes-Moorhouse** VC (XV108 – later ZA148)
**Arthur Scarf** VC (XV109 – later ZA147)
**Leonard Cheshire** VC (ZD241)

represent all of his Bomber Command colleagues.

The result was a list of fourteen VC holders who then lent their names to the RAF's first 14 VC10s, and these are shown in the accompanying box. The first aircraft (XR810) was unveiled at RAF Brize Norton, Oxfordshire on November 11, 1968 and in a special ceremony it was named 'David Lord VC' by the late pilot's brother. Relatives of ten of the 15 VC holders were also present at the event.

When the early VC10s were retired the 'names' subsequently transferred to the 14 newer Super VC10 K.3 and K.4 variants and these were carried until the type was finally withdrawn in 2013. When airframes were gradually scrapped the surviving examples took on the extra names, so as to keep all the VC holder's tributes aloft.  When ZA147 made the type's last flight on September 25, 2013 it actually carried five name scrolls on its nose; thus bringing to a conclusion a tradition that had started 45 years previously.

Some of the RAF VC10s survived to be preserved by museums and although the name 'scrolls' were removed before delivery most have had this important part of their history returned by their new owners. In fact, VC10 K.3 ZA148 (now at Newquay, Cornwall) has been repainted with the names of all the VC holders previously worn on the entire fleet.

## 'Living' Memorials

Over the years the dramatic stories behind the award of a Victoria Cross have tempted the operators of various flyable vintage 'warbirds' to paint their aircraft in markings representing those of an award recipient.

In the 1980s the RAF's Battle of Britain Memorial Flight (BBMF) painted Hawker Hurricane LF363 in the GN-A markings of James Nicolson's 249 Sqn aircraft and when 44 Sqn transferred 'it's' Avro Lancaster to the BBMF in 1973 it was painted in the KM-B markings flown by 44 Sqn's John Nettleton at the time of his VC.

When it was restored to fly in 1987 the British Aerial Museum's Bristol Blenheim IV G-MKIV was painted to represent Hughie Edwards' V6028/GB-D. Sadly the aircraft, which was actually a Canadian-built Bolingbroke, was destroyed less than a month later in a forced landing.

F/O John Cruickshank's VC winning Consolidated PBY-5 Catalina JV928 formed the basis for the colour scheme worn by Plane Sailing Air Displays' Super Catalina G-BLSC in the 1980s and early 1990s. This aircraft was ultimately repainted into a different scheme and re-registered in Bermuda but was lost in an accident in Southampton Harbour in 1998.

The Canadian Warplane Heritage Museum flies its Canso (C-FPQL) in the colours of David Hornell's VC winning aircraft complete with 9754/P markings *Doug Fisher*

Albert Ball is commemorated in his native Nottingham.  This statue stands in the grounds of Nottingham Castle and his medal and assorted memorabilia are displayed within the city's museum *Steve Bridgewater*

Albert Ball's medals on display in the City of Nottingham Museum alongside a windscreen removed from his aircraft and thought to come from an experimental SE5a used by Ball while serving with 56 Sqn *Steve Bridgewater*

Another Catalina – the former Greenpeace-operated N423RS – also wore Cruickshank's markings while in the UK. However, this aircraft only flew three times between 1998 and 2015 and has since been shipped (by boat) to the USA for restoration.

A 'Cat' already operates in the markings of a VC holder on the west side of the Atlantic Ocean. The Canadian Warplane Heritage Museum (CWHM) in Hamilton, Ontario flies its Canso (C-FPQL) in the colours of David Hornell's VC winning aircraft complete with 9754/P markings.

The CWHM Avro Lancaster X (FM213/C-GVRA) also famously flies in the markings of F/O Andrew Mynarski's KB726/VR-A of 419 Sqn. This airframe was acquired by the museum in 1977 and was restored to airworthy condition over eleven years before returning to the skies on September 24, 1988.

Fellow Canadian operator Vintage Wings of Canada also pays tribute to

a Canadian VC holder. The collection's Chance Vought FG.1D Corsair (C-GVWC) – which won the 2003 EAA AirVenture Grand Champion Warbird award and previously flew in 22 episodes of the Blacksheep Squadron TV series – is painted to represent Robert Hampton Gray's KD658/115.

Back in the UK the 2015 season saw the two extremes of aviation honouring VC recipients – to mark the 75th anniversary of the Battle of Britain the RAF's 29 Sqn painted Eurofighter Typhoon ZK349 into the GN-A codes worn by James Nicolson's Hurricane and to commemorate the centenary of William Rhodes-Moorhouse wining the first airborne VC the Great War Display Team's replica Royal Aircraft Factory BE.2 (owned and flown by Matthew Boddington) flew in the markings of his '687.'

More than a century after British and Commonwealth pilots began receiving the Victoria Cross the 51 recipients are far from forgotten.

**Left:** The British Aerial Museum's Bristol Bolingbroke, flying in the markings of Hughie Edwards' Blenheim IV in 1987
**Right:** Matthew Boddington's BE.2 replica at IWM Duxford in 2016. The aircraft is painted to represent the aircraft flown by William Rhodes-Moorhouse when he became the first pilot to receive a **VC** *Steve Bridgewater*

## INDEX OF VC WINNING AVIATORS

| Name | Type | Reg | Codes | Date of Action | Date of Medal* | Location of Medal |
|---|---|---|---|---|---|---|
| William Rhodes Moorhouse | BE.2b | 687 | - | April 22, 1915 | May 22, 1915 | Lord Ashcroft VC Collection/IWM |
| Reginald Warneford | Morane L | 3253 | - | June 7, 1915 | June 11, 1915 | Fleet Air Arm Museum |
| Lanoe Hawker | Airco DH.2 | 5964 | - | July 25, 1915 | August 24, 1915 | Royal Air Force Museum |
| John Liddell | RE.5 | 2457 | - | July 31, 1915 | August 23, 1915 | Lord Ashcroft VC Collection/IWM |
| Gilbert Insall | Vickers FB.5 | 5074 | - | November 7, 1915 | December 23, 1915 | Royal Air Force Museum |
| Richard Bell-Davies | Nieuport 12 | 3172 | - | November 19, 1915 | December 31, 1915 | Fleet Air Arm Museum |
| Lionel Brabazon Rees | Airco DH.2 | 6015 | - | July 1, 1916 | October 29, 1916 | Lord Ashcroft VC Collection/IWM |
| William Leefe-Robinson | BE.2c | 2693 | - | September 3, 1916 | September 5, 1916 | Lord Ashcroft VC Collection/IWM |
| Thomas Mottershead | FE.2d | A39 | - | January 7, 1917 | February 12, 1917 | Lord Ashcroft VC Collection/IWM |
| Frank McNamara | Martinsyde | 7486 | - | March 20, 1917 | June 8, 1917 | Royal Air Force Museum |
| William 'Billy' Bishop | Nieuport 17 | B1566 | C-5 | June 2, 1917 | August 11, 1917 | Canadian War Museum |
| Albert Ball | SE.5 | A8898 | - | May/June 1917 | June 8, 1917 | City of Nottingham Museum |
| Alan McLeod | F.K.8 | B5773 | - | March 27, 1918 | May 1, 1918 | Canadian War Museum |
| Alan Jerrard | Camel | B5648 | E | March 30, 1918 | April 30, 1918 | Lord Ashcroft VC Collection/IWM |
| James McCudden | SE.5a | B4863 | G | Early 1918 | March 29, 1918 | Royal Engineers Museum |
| Ferdinand West | F.K.8 | C8594 | - | August 9, 1918 | November 8, 1918 | Imperial War Museum |
| William Barker | Snipe | E8102 | | October 27, 1918 | November 30, 1918 | Canadian War Museum |
| Andrew Beauchamp Proctor | SE.5 | D6856 | Various | November 30, 1918 | | Lord Ashcroft VC Collection/IWM |
| Edward Mannock | SE.5 | B4484 | Various | July 18, 1919 | | Lord Ashcroft VC Collection/IWM |
| Donald Garland | Battle | P2204 | PH-K | May 12, 1940 | June 11, 19140 | Royal Air Force Museum |
| Thomas Gray | Battle | P2204 | PH-K | May 12, 1940 | June 11, 19140 | Privately Owne |
| Roderick Learoyd | Hampden | P4403 | EA-M | August 12, 1940 | August 20, 1940 | Lord Ashcroft VC Collection/IWM |
| Eric 'James' Nicolson | Hurricane | P3376 | GN-A | August 16, 1940 | November 15, 1940 | Royal Air Force Museum |
| John Hannah | Hampden | P1355 | OL-W | September 15, 1940 | October 1, 1940 | Royal Air Force Museum |
| Kenneth Campbell | Beaufort | N1016 | OA-X | April 6, 1941 | March 13, 1942 | 22 Sqn Museum, RAF |
| Hughie Edwards | Blenheim IV | V6028 | GB-D | July 4, 1941 | July 22, 1941 | Australian War Memorial |
| James Ward | Wellington | L7818 | AA-R | July 7, 1941 | August 5, 1941 | Auckland War Memorial Museum |
| Arthur Scarf | Blenheim I | L1134 | PT-F | December 9, 1941 | June 21, 1946 | Royal Air Force Museum |
| Eugene Esmonde | Swordfish I | W5984 | H | February 12, 1942 | March 3, 1942 | Imperial War Museum |
| John Nettleton | Lancaster | R5508 | KM-B | April 17, 1942 | April 24, 1942 | Privately Owned |
| Leslie Manser | Manchester | L7301 | ZN-D | May 30, 1942 | October 20, 1942 | Lord Ashcroft VC Collection/IWM |
| 'Ron' Middleton | Stirling | BF372 | OJ-H | November 28, 1942 | January 15, 1943 | Australian War Memorial |
| Hugh Malcolm | Blenheim V | BA875 | WV-V | December 4, 1942 | April 27, 1943 | Lord Ashcroft VC Collection/IWM |
| William Newton | Boston | RAAF A28-3 | DU-Y | March 16, 1943 | October 19. 1943 | Australian War Memorial |
| Leonard Trent | Ventura | AJ209 | EG-V | May 3, 1943 | February 26, 1946 | Air Force Museum of New Zealand |
| Guy Gibson | Lancaster (S) | ED932 | AJ-G | May 17, 1943 | May 28, 1943 | Royal Air Force Museum |
| Lloyd Trigg | Liberator V | BZ832 | D | August 11, 1943 | November 2, 1943 | Lord Ashcroft VC Collection/IWM |
| Arthur Aaron | Stirling | EF452 | HA-O | August 12, 1943 | November 5, 1943 | Leeds City Museum |
| William Reid | Lancaster | LM360 | WS-O | November 3, 1943 | December 14, 1943 | Privately Owned (Melissa John) |
| Cyril Barton | Halifax | LK797 | EY-E | March 30, 1944 | June 27, 1944 | Royal Air Force Museum |
| Norman Jackson | Lancaster | ME669 | ZN-O | April 26, 1944 | October 26, 1945 | Lord Ashcroft VC Collection/IWM |
| Andrew Mynarski | Lancaster | KB726 | VR-A | June 12, 1944 | October 8, 1946 | 1 Canadian Air Division |
| David Hornell | Canso | RCAF 9754 | P | June 24, 1944 | July 25, 1944 | 1 Canadian Air Division |
| John Cruickshank | Catalina | JV928 | DA-Y | July 17, 1944 | September 1, 1944 | Privately Owned (J Cruickshank) |
| Ian Bazalgette | Lancaster | ND811 | F2-T | August 4, 1944 | August 14, 1945 | Royal Air Force Museum |
| 'Leonard' Cheshire | Various | - | | Various | September 8, 1944 | Imperial War Museum |
| David Lord | Dakota III | KG374 | YS-L | September 19, 1944 | November 9, 1945 | Lord Ashcroft VC Collection/IWM |
| Robert Palmer | Lancaster | PB371 | 60-V | December 23, 1944 | March 20, 1945 | Privately Owned |
| George Thompson | Lancaster | PD377 | WS-U | January 1, 1945 | February 16, 1945 | National War Museum of Scotland |
| Edwin Swales | Lancaster | PB538 | 60-M | February 23, 1945 | April 24, 1945 | Johannesburg Museum of Military History |
| Robert Hampton Gray | Corsair IV | KD658 | 115 | August 9, 1945 | August 21, 1945 | Privately Owned |

* Date of the London Gazette in which the award was promulgated